The Five Inch Course
Thinking Your Way To Better Golf

By John Lloyd Retzer

www.golfblogger.com

For My Wife, Who Puts Up With My Golf Addiction

"Competitive golf is played on a five and a half inch course – the space between your ears."

Bobby Jones

Table of Contents

Introduction

In 1960, the average golf score was 100. Fifty years later, with all the innovations in clubs, balls and instruction, the average golf score is ... still 100. In fact, only 20 percent of all golfers will ever (honestly) break that mark.

More bad news: Barring a major investment in time and money, you're stuck with the swing you have. Tips from golf magazines, your buddies -- even the occasional lesson from a pro-- aren't going to result in long term improvement. Studies have shown that most players never get better than they are five years into their golfing "career."

However, this doesn't mean that lower scores are out of your reach. It just means that you have to play better golf with the swing you already have.

Note that I said "better golf," not "better golf swing." The weekend player, I think, often confuses the two. The singular goal of golf is to get the ball in the hole in the fewest number of strokes. It matters not how you get that done. Four ugly strokes equal four pretty ones.

As a high school golf coach, I found that in a few short weeks I could take absolute beginners (and I often had these to fill up my roster) and teach them to work their way around the course in something approaching respectability. A kid who had never held a club in their life would break 50 (we played nine-hole competitions) in a couple of weeks.

But here's the kicker: Those rank beginners would break 50 while rarely taking a full swing. Instead, they'd pitch, chip and putt their way around the course with a variety of clubs. A long putting stroke with a 3 wood rolls the ball a hundred and ten or 20 yards down the fairway. Do that three times, and you're on or near the green on a par 4. A pitch or chip with a high numbered iron puts you on the green, and a couple of putts -- the easiest stroke to learn -- gets you in the hole. Do that on nine holes and you card a 54. Get a couple of breaks and you're inside of 50.

Remember that the average golf score is 100 - - 50 for nine. Without taking a full swing, these beginners sometimes could score better than average -- because unlike the average player, they kept the ball in the fairway, stayed away from trouble and worked methodically toward the goal. They didn't have to extract themselves from the woods because they generally didn't hit the ball that far. They didn't hit five-yard chunks. And they didn't shank.

The pitch, chip and putt method is ugly but effective. It also was necessary. As the team's solitary coach, there wasn't time to teach the fine points of a full swing to five or six beginners while working with the better players who constituted the Varsity and JV. All I could hope was that those beginners would get excited enough about their early success (occasionally scoring better than players on the JV) to get some lessons on their own and practice in the off season.

As coach, I also discovered that working with my better players' swings during the season could be disastrous. There just wasn't enough time in a short season for any swing changes to become second nature. Before a change becomes second nature, a player's scores often will go up (look at the impact swing changes had on Tiger Woods' game). Swing changes were best left to the long offseason when a player could spend considerable time at the range grooving a new move.

Between beginners who couldn't swing, and better players whose swings I didn't want to touch, my focus as a coach turned to getting my players to score better with the swings they brought into the season. And that required playing smarter, not swinging better.

That's when I began collecting these notes on playing smarter golf. In a series of notebooks, on my Palm Pilot (now a Blackberry) and in various computer files, I recorded my own observations, advice from other coaches and tips from books and magazines. I made playing smarter the focus of both my coaching and my own golf game.

A frequent playing partner once observed that I'm a 13 handicapper with the swing of a 25. I hit for average distance and make my share of bad swings. But I don't make many mental mistakes. I know my limitations and play well within them. Playing high percentage golf, I can get around a course in fewer strokes than players who are bombing it 40 yards past me (usually 40 yards past me into the woods). Another partner says I play "old man golf."

For players who don't have lots of spare time and money, playing better golf means playing smarter golf. The typical weekend golfer can take as many as ten strokes off his score simply by making intelligent decisions about distances, targets and club selection. It requires thinking and mental discipline. But in the end, that's easier to change than your swing.

So here -- collected in book form -- are my notes on playing smarter golf. They have helped my game. I know they will help yours.

Remember Bobby Jones' dictum: Competitive Golf Is Played On A Five And A Half Inch Course – The Space Between Your Ears.

How To Use This Book

The Five Inch Course consists of a collection of (generally) short mental game tips, organized into chapters of related thoughts:

- Before You Play

- From Tee To Green

- On Every Shot

- On The Tee

- In The Fairway

- Off The Fairway

- Around The Green

- On The Green

- After the Round

Don't try to memorize all these tips and put them into play next time out. Instead, read through the book and pick a couple that speak to problems you've noticed in your own game. Once you incorporate those, add a couple more. After a few rounds, you'll find playing the Five Inch Course is second nature.

That said, a few tips need immediate consideration:

- Know Your Distances

- Know The Difference Between Carry and Roll

- Work On Your Alignment

- Pick A Target

- Play Conservatively

Of these, the admonition to know your distances is most important. If you don't have an honest assessment of how far you hit the ball with each club, you'll never score any better.

It's probably not possible to put all of the tips in the Five Inch Course into play all the time. I've been working on this volume for years, and still manage to lose my concentration and play shots without thinking them through. Sometimes, I'll get distracted and play a whole series of unthinking shots. That's when I start getting into real trouble.

In the end, remember this one idea:

It's okay to hit bad shots, but hitting a stupid one is unforgivable.

Before You Play

*Improving your game begins before you get to the course.
As with all things in life, Proper Prior Planning
Prevents Poor Performance.*

Stay Focused On The Goal

Keep your eye on the ball (pun intended) and your scoring will improve. It is worth repeating that the single goal of golf is to get the ball into the hole in as few strokes as possible. Anything else is an unnecessary distraction.

So park the ego and forget about holding an unspoken long drive contest with your playing partners. Forget about the flop that Phil hit last week. Don't worry about what club you "should" be hitting; use the one that will do the job.

Play what my friends refer to as "old man golf." The senior citizens in our league always seem to be among the leaders in scoring. These guys barely hit it 180 off the tee, use a 5 iron from 140, and have been known to putt balls out of a sand trap. They play ugly. And yet at the end of almost every round, they're in contention.

I think it's because they've reached the age where there's no need to try to impress anyone. They are focused on getting the ball into the hole as quickly as possible.

Don't Let Yourself Get Suckered Into An Ego Competition

Getting suckered into an undeclared long drive or irons contest with your playing partners will drive up your score. Play your own game.

I am not a long hitter, but my easy swing will nearly always keep the ball in play. The minute I go for extra distance, I send the ball into the rough or out-of-bounds, costing precious strokes. I have to remind myself of this when playing with my big hitting friends. They may outdrive me by 30 yards from the tee, but when the round is over, my score is always just as good or better.

Know Your Distances

The admonition to know how far you hit your clubs seems too obvious for words, but the fact of the matter is that most amateurs really don't know. A study from a few years ago showed that while the average golfer thinks he hits the driver 230 yards, he actually averages around 200. Similar distance miscalculations hold true throughout the bag.

Too often we see our golf game through rose colored glasses. Because we once hit a 6 iron 170 yards, we have convinced ourselves that's our natural distance with that club. What we don't remember is that nine times out of ten it goes more like 150.

If you don't know with a fair degree of accuracy how far each club goes, you will constantly make errors in judgment that will cost you strokes.

In years past, getting a good read on your distances was real work. The most common method was to take a shag bag to an open field, hit a bunch of balls and then take measurements with a long tape measure or by pacing it out. I actually did that on several occasions and collected a fair amount of data, but the whole process was rather inconvenient.

These days, even the most basic GPS units will let you measure shot distances. Another option is to go to a local driving range that has a radar system, set up and hit several buckets of balls. This, however, is not as good an option for several reasons. First, hitting a ball off a plastic mat is not the equivalent of hitting off grass and dirt. Second, unless you play with driving range balls, your own ball likely will perform differently.

In any case, whether you pace off distances, measure with a GPS or rely on driving range radar, you should begin to collect data on your shots. Try to get ten distances per club. Toss the top and bottom two as outliers and then average the rest.

Write the distances for each club on a small piece of paper and then tape it to the back of a bag tag. Alternately, put a small sticker with the distance on the shaft of each club. Either way, you'll have a handy reference to your real distances until they become second nature.

Then — and this is the hardest part — pay attention to the measurements on the course.

Know The Difference Between Carry and Roll

Related to the previous entries about knowing your distance is the notion of knowing the difference between your carry and roll. Carry is the distance your ball travels through the air, while roll is the forward progress it makes upon landing. Having a good idea about your carry and roll can save you critical strokes when facing a hazard, rough or waste area.

Suppose that you are standing on a tee, needing a 200-yard carry to negotiate a large swamp (a typical shot at my local courses in southeastern Michigan). The reflect response is to pull out the driver and have a go. But that may not be wise. If you hit your driver 240 yards, of which 200 is carry and 40 roll, you're likely to catch the edge of the hazard — and may even bounce back in. A ball struck off the driver will come in low those last several yards, perhaps even bringing the tops of cattails into play.

For this task, you might want to consider a higher-lofted club — one with less overall distance, but more carry. In my case, a 5 wood that goes 210, of which virtually all is carry, is the better choice. The overall distance is much less, but there's no chance of catching the tops of the cattails or the swamp bank, and losing strokes.

It also helps to know your carry and roll when making an approach shot over a trap or similar greenside hazard. In those instances, you need to ensure not only that you've got the correct distance, but also the correct carry. Roll doesn't do any good when your ball is stymied by a steep walled trap.

Figuring your carry and roll is a bit more difficult than figuring your overall distance. The best advice is to take a good look at the ball in flight and try to get a fix on the landing spot. Then, when measuring the overall distance, use that as an intermediate point. After collecting this data, record the final results on the same note that you're using to record overall distances and shot shapes.

Finally, there's the usual bit of warning: none of these tips will do any good at all if you don't put them into play.

Know Your Tendencies

As important as knowing your distance is knowing your tendencies. I'm always amazed when a playing partner steps up to the tee, plants his ball in the center, and announces: "Look out. I have no idea where this is going." Often as not, the high-handicapper takes a mighty swing and slices the ball into the tree line. It's probably the same result eight out of ten times.

Rare indeed is the player whose swing is so erratic that he truly has no idea where the ball is headed. More likely, the weekend warrior is either delusional, or uninformed.

The delusional player knows he's going to slice (or pop it up or hook or whatever), but has convinced himself otherwise (because he once in a great while hits a ball that behaves). A related delusion says that even though it's always a slice, THIS time, I'll figure out the magic move and drive it right down the middle. This player has simply never thought seriously about his game and really doesn't have a clue.

Knowing your ball flight tendencies can save you pile of strokes on the course. If nine times out of ten you slice a club, you can plan for that by aiming to compensate. Similarly, when lying behind a line of trees, it pays to know which club will carry you over the leaves.

The solution to knowing what your ball is going to do is to collect raw data. The next time you play, ask the appropriate questions. Does your driver slice, draw, fade or hook? How high does it fly? What does the 3 wood do? The 5 iron? Your pitching wedge?

Chances are that your shot shape varies from club to club. One will induce you to a low draw, while another consistently slices. I tend to slice my longer clubs, except for the driver, which I hit with a fade or a hook. The shorter clubs also trend toward a fade. Knowing how each club tends to perform will allow you to choose the correct tool for each job.

As you play your next few rounds, keep track of the ball's flight path. Note both the shape of the horizontal flight and also of the height. I found that a good way to do this is to draw a sketch of each shot on the illustration of the hole on my scorecard. This method allows for quite a bit of post round analysis.

The trick, as with most mental golf tips, is to actually remember to put them into play. If you already have a handy card with your club distances recorded, include a note about each club's shot shape. Then, when setting up to take your shots, remember to play your percentages.

Keep A Yardage Book

If you're a regular on a particular course, keep a yardage book. Pros keep yardage books and notes on each Tour course; you should develop one for your favorites.

Store a small note book in your bag -- I like the reporter's style that's hinged at the top -- for making sketches of the holes and taking notes on what works and what doesn't. Draw large illustrations of the greens and make notes on how each plays, with arrows indicating the fall lines. Note how the holes play under different conditions, blind spots, danger zones and safe plays. You also could note the clubs used from particular areas.

Then, before teeing it up, consult your notebook and refresh your memory. Use the book to avoid repeating mistakes.

Keep A Golf Diary

Keeping a golf diary is not only a means to better play, but also a nice way to reminisce.

After each round, record the vitals: the course name and location; its par, slope and rating; weather and course conditions and your score. Make notes on your favorite and least-favorite holes; your best-played hole and shot; and your worst hole and shot. Identify areas of weakness, such as failing to get out of the sand, or missing too many fairways. Finally, make notes on what you will do differently when next you play the course.

Notes like these can help you think clearly about a round after the exhaustion and jubilation (or anger) subsides. The "favorites and best" entries offer positive visualization; the "least and worst," future focus areas.

Just as important, a golf journal offers continuity in what otherwise might become a disjointed mash of individual rounds.

There actually are some commercial golf diaries available, but you obviously can use any sort of notebook. My own is a reporter's style notebook from Moleskine.

Learn From Your Mistakes

It's perfectly acceptable to make mistakes on the course. What's not acceptable is making the same mistakes over and again.

A fellow that I play with has a terrible time with the driver off the tee. His iron play, on the other hand is terrific. He can hit an accurate 3 iron well over 200 yards. I've suggested a couple of times that he would play better if he hit an iron off the tee. With his length, he can easily hit greens in regulation with irons alone. But he insists on using a driver off the tee, spraying it into the trees and losing shots. His scores are not getting any lower.

In your golf journal -- you are keeping one, aren't you? -- make a note of the things you repeatedly do poorly. And make a note to change your behavior -- or at the very least to practice them at the next opportunity.

Temper Your Expectations

You are not a tour player (although I can think of a couple of Tour players who would do well to read these tips) and thus need to reign in your expectations. You are not going to make par or birdie on every hole (or perhaps even most), and are going to hit more than your share of bad shots.

Get over it.

Having realistic expectations can help you score better. In the aftermath of a poor play, make note of what went wrong, and then concentrate on the next shot. There's no need to beat yourself up. You've made bad shots in the past -- and you're going to make more in the future. Getting angry about the inevitable increases tension and makes poor play more likely as the round goes on.

Set a realistic goal for yourself before setting out. If you consistently shoot over 100, set the goal of breaking the century mark. If you consistently shoot in the low 90s, use 89 as your mark. Be sure, however, to adjust your goal for the course. If your goal is to break 90 for the first time, and you're trying it on a new course that has a 135 slope, you're in for a day of unrealized expectations.

One of the funniest (and saddest) things I know is the weekender who works himself into a raging fury after a poor shot. "I can't believe I hit that shot," he rages -- and I think: "Why not? You've been hitting them like that all day long."

"Every golfer scores better when he learns his capabilities." - Tommy Armour

Get A Clubfitting

Players in the market for a new set of clubs are on a fool's errand if they don't get a professional clubfitting. By measuring — and then accounting for — your height, weight, age, flexibility, swing speed, angle of attack, stance and other factors, a good clubfitter can get you into a set of clubs that will maximize the game you already have.

If you've already got a set of clubs, never fear. For a reasonable fee, a clubfitter generally can take measurements and adjust your club's loft and lie, shaft length and swingweight. More drastically — but still cheaper than replacing a set of clubs — a clubfitter can swap out your current shafts with ones more suited to your game. A clubfitter also can get you fitted for grips.

A few rules of thumb about clubfitting:

- Lie Angle: The Lie Angle is the angle formed by the shaft when the sole rests on the ground. A club that stands too upright for a golfer will tend to cause a pull, or hook. A club that is too flat encourages a slice.
- Shaft Length: The longer the club, the flatter the lie angle.
- Loft: Loft is the angle of the face. It affects trajectory, spin and carry. Knowing a manufacturer's loft and lie specs can be useful, but they're affected by how you hold your club. Players who set up with their hands forward effectively "deloft" their clubs. Loft also can be affected by the angle at which a player brings his clubs through the hitting zone.
- Shaft Flex: A shaft that is too stiff for a player can reduce distance and make shots tend right. A shaft that is too flexible can result in club spraying, as well as added height to a shot (possibly reducing distance).
- Grips: Grips that are too large can encourage a hook. Grips that are too small can encourage a slice.

In any event, the key here is that a good clubfitting can actually improve your game without your making a swing change. It's about maximizing the swing your already have.

Evaluate Your Club Collection

The clubs you put into your bag make a difference. Thanks — or no thanks — to the influence of the manufacturers and the pros, the typical weekender I see carries a driver, putter, 3-PW, SW, two woods and a specialty wedge — often a sixty degree model, but sometimes a gap wedge.

It's worth thinking seriously about which clubs you carry, which you use, and which you might need. Your bag should reflect your unique game, not some pre-determined set.

When tracking your distances and shot tendencies, also pay attention to the clubs you use most often. It's likely that there are a couple of clubs in your bag that you use once a round or less. Another possibility is that there are two clubs that overlap in terms of distance. If either of these is the case, it makes sense to substitute something with a little more utility.

Dropping a little-used long iron for another wedge is a typical move. It's also eminently sensible. Half and three-quarter wedge shots are tricky and adding a club to fill in a distance gap can save shots. If chipping is a weakness, you might drop an unused club for a specialty chipper.

For others, dropping the driver would be a bold, but practical move. Studies have repeatedly shown that weekenders typically hit their 3 wood just as far — if not further — than their driver. If you're one of those, get rid of the big dog and add a scoring club.

Later, if you're on the course and find you need the missing club — say, a 4 iron — take a longer stick and either choke down or swing easy. (But for heavens sake, don't take a shorter club and swing harder).

Players who have thought seriously about their set often end up with unusual combinations. On fellow I played with had no driver, but carried two putters: one, he explained, was for long shots; the other for short ones. Another, perhaps running counter to conventional wisdom, dropped the fairway woods — which he did not hit effectively — in favor of a couple of wedges with different bounce angles.

The point is to treat your clubs like a set of tools — and to carry the tools that are most likely to help you accomplish the task at hand: getting the ball into the hole.

Play Game Improvement Clubs

There's absolutely nothing like the feel of a golf ball striking the sweet spot on a forged iron. And there's no satisfaction like being able to work the ball left and right into a green at will.

That said, most of us do well to just consistently hit the ball in the air, straight and with decent distance. Do that every time and your scores will come down.

Game Improvement and Super Game Improvement Irons incorporate a variety of technologies designed to do exactly what you need: get the ball in the air, straight, with decent distance. Offset helps a player close the face in time; cavity backs stabilize the clubhead (increase moment of inertia); weight redistribution helps to get the ball in the air more consistently. Lighter shafts, hollow bodies and multi-material construction all are employed in the name of consistently straight and in the air with decent distance.

Club snobs argue that game improvement clubs don't offer enough feedback, and that your game may never improve if you stick to the "higher handicapper" lines. That may be true, but your average weekender doesn't practice enough to be able to appreciate the difference.

Play the clubs that will make the best of the swing you have. If you don't have a muscleback swing, don't play them.

As of late, even Tour players are buying into the improvement club logic. Look into the bags of many current pros and you will find they've traded traditional long irons for cavity backs, hybrids and other game changers. A recent study revealed that only 30 percent of tour pros play the traditional muscleback blades.

Play An Appropriate Ball

We live in the Golden Age of the golf ball. Breakthroughs in design, materials and manufacturing have produced a bumper crop. No matter what your body type, swing style or clubhead speed, there's a ball specifically designed for you.

Unfortunately, far too many players give absolutely no thought to the ball they play. In a pro shop, they instinctively reach for the Pro V1 because that's the ball that has won the marketing race. Everyone is convinced that it's the best ball on the market — and it may be. But a ball that pros and top amateurs love with their 100+ mph swing speeds may not be the best ball for you.

A critical factor in golf ball performance is compression. At impact, the golf ball is flattened against the face of the club, and then rebounds into its original shape. You can see this quite clearly in slow motion television analyses of tour players' swings.

To get the most distance (and accuracy) out of your ball, it needs to be just soft enough for you to achieve that compression. Compressing a ball too much or too little can be counterproductive.

All things being equal, a player with a higher swing speed will be able to crush a higher compression ball more easily. It follows, then, that a ball favored by fast swinging pros and top amateurs may be a little too hard for slower swinging weekenders.

There are other factors, too. Design and composition of balls lead to varying spin rates. Spin and the dimples create loft and carry. Slower-swinging golfers may need higher spin rates for greater distance. But greater spin also can create hooks and slices. An erratic ball striker may need one with lower spin.

The short game also factors into this. Players who are adept at high flying short games will require a different ball than those who prefer the pitch-and-run.

Feel with the putter is another consideration. While improved manufacturing tolerances ensure that virtually every ball these days is "true," their feel off the putter can be quite different. I've rejected a couple of otherwise good balls for no reason other than they didn't "feel" right off the putter. All of this makes the choice of a golf ball a somewhat complex decision.

(To appreciate how far things have come, consider this: Through the 1970s, tour pros would carry a metal ring on their bag, sized perfectly for a golf ball. Before putting a new ball into play, they would pass it through the ring to ensure that it was correctly sized and shaped.)

A recent development in golf balls is the notion of a golf ball fitting. These are generally available at the national golf chain stores, high end local pro shops and at better equipped golf learning centers. The computerized equipment will track your swing speed, launch angle, ball spin rate and other factors and compare it to data on known balls to give you a "best fit."

Barring a ball fitting, your best bet is to try a variety of balls based on what you know about your own swing and manufacturer's claims. Balls advertised as "low compression" generally are best for those with slower swing speeds. Those that claim to reduce hooks and slices typically are lower spin models.

The biggest barrier to picking a ball without professional help is estimating your swing speed. You can get a rough estimate of your swing speed from your 150 yard club. If that Club is a 6 or a 7 iron, your swing is in the 80 - 90 mph range; if it's between a 7 and an eight, 90 - 100; an 8 to a 9 iron would indicate a 100+ swing speed. Another rule of thumb is to divide the number of yards of carry with your driver by 2.3.

Finally, be aware — as I'm sure you are — that ball price has little to do with which one is best for your game. There are some absolutely superb balls for under $20 a dozen aimed precisely at slower swinging weekenders.

Adjust Your Bag For The Course

A few years back, I spent a day at the Buick Open hanging out in the TaylorMade equipment van. It was a busy place, as seemingly endless stream of golf pros arrived (often on multiple occasions) to have their clubs tweaked for that week's playing conditions.

Most just wanted an adjustment in loft and lie (TaylorMade could do this even on their metal woods — a neat technical trick); a couple, however, wanted a major change: a different shaft, head or a new club entirely. (One even wanted TaylorMade to put together a special putter with a flag grip that he could give as a gift to the President of the United States, with whom he was having lunch the following week).

The lesson is obvious one: that the course and its conditions should dictate the makeup of the clubs in your bag. Very few of us have the money or skills to do constant adjustments to loft and lie or to routinely swap out heads and shafts. On the other hand, nearly every golfer I know has spare clubs sitting in the garage that with a little local knowledge can be used to tweak their bags for better results.

During the passage of a season, I regularly play two different courses, each of which calls for a slightly different club mix. The first is a traditional course with parallel fairways, and no rough to speak of. Instead, the unwatered areas outside the fairways run very hard with very short scrub. On that layout, I typically set aside my long irons and add a 7 and 9 wood and a rescue style "6." Because I can't possibly dig the club into the ground, the flatter bottomed "woods" are more effective.

The other track is mostly a prairie course, with thick rough and foot tall prairie grasses guarding the edges. Here, I find that I need the long irons because the woods cannot cut through the grass to move the ball along.

Distances also factor into my thinking. On the course my league plays, there's a par 3 that for me absolutely requires a 5 iron. I never use it on most other courses. That same track finds me with a hybrid in the bag—not necessarily for full swings, but for the bump and run shots I can use to get the ball to the green from the fairway, and from out of the rough under unkempt tree branches.

I also know a guy who carries two putters on a particular course because the greens are so large that he needs a "lag" putter and a "close" putter.

Before heading out to your favorite course in the future, think seriously about how your club mix fits with the course design.

Dress Appropriately

One of the earliest pieces of advice my Pro friend gave me was to dress well. His feeling was that if you were dressed like a "player," you'd feel like one and that would carry over to your game.

I think he's right. Golf is such a mental game that anything that can keep you in the moment is worth trying. Playing in jeans and a tank top just doesn't lead to the same mental state as a golf shirt and neatly pressed Bermudas (as an aside, I'm in favor of federal legislation banning the wearing of tank tops in public by anyone over 21).

But there's more to apparel than that. Today's specialized golf wear is designed to keep you cool and comfortable through moisture wicking fabrics. It's cut to allow a free swing. Some companies are experimenting with shirts that can actually help improve your swing.

Footwear also is important. You can't play well if your feet hurt. Golf shoes now are designed with the latest athletic shoe technology. There even are "climate controlled" socks; others have extra padding in places critical to the golf swing.

In cooler weather, dress in light layers. As the sun warms the day, you can shed layers to remain comfortable. And once again, the miracle of modern fabrics comes through. Lighter, warmer, moisture wicking fabrics will keep you playing well into the fall, and in the early spring.

Dress for golf. Even if you don't play better, you'll feel better.

Clean Or Replace Your Grips

Your grips are the connection to the golf club. So it makes sense to do a little maintenance on them. Worn, slippery grips can cause you to grasp the club too firmly, resulting in tension and other bad results. Fortunately, regripping is easy if you use rubber slip on grips:

1) Cut off the old grips with a utility knife. For safety's sake – and to keep from scratching your shafts – use a hook blade.

2) Strip off the old tape. Use a hair dryer to melt the glue if the tape is stubborn.

3) Get some double sided grip tape from Golfsmith or Golfworks.

4) Secure the club in a vice with soft rubber clamps. You can get ones designed for golf clubs from Golfworks or Golfsmith.

5) Apply the tape: There are two ways to do this: You can start at the lower end of where the grip would be by running it in a spiral pattern up the shaft. Or, you can run it lengthwise up one side of the butt and down the other. Peel the backing off the tape so the stick side is revealed. You may find it easier if you precut the tape.

6) Put another small strip over the hole on the butt.

7) Put something to catch the mineral spirits under the butt end. I use an aluminum paint tray for paint rollers.

8) Pour some mineral spirits into the grip while holding your finger over the hole at the bottom. Slosh the spirits around inside the grip.

9) Pour the spirits from the inside of the grip over the tape. Add a little bit more of the spirits until the glue on the tape is slick.

10) Push the grip onto the shaft.

11) Most grips have a couple of little marks at the top and bottom ends to help with alignment.

Make sure that these align with each other. Otherwise, the grip might be slightly twisted, which may affect your swing.

12) You can put the logo up (I do), or down (as many pros do). Just make sure that the marks line up parallel to the shaft.

Clean Your Grooves

One of the simplest things you can do to improve your scores is to keep your club faces clean. It's no accident that professional caddies wipe their players' clubs after every shot. And yet so many weekenders will play an entire round while only bothering to knock off the obvious clumps.

Grooves that are free of dirt and grass particles will impart a more consistent spin to the ball. A consistent spin will produce more accuracy. Nice clean grooves and high spin also will help a ball stop quickly on the green.

There are so many gadgets and tools on the market to clean your clubs and grooves that it would be impossible to catalog them all. There are special towels, brushes in hundreds of shapes and sizes, foaming cleansers, pick tools and on and on.

I use one of the simplest—and cheapest—methods: a rough towel. I get the end of the towel a little damp before heading out and then hang it from my bag. Wiping the club face first with the damp end, and then with the dry works 99% of the time. If things get stubborn, I have a golf pocket knife in the bag with a groove gouging tool.

Arrive Early

One of the sayings my students most hate to hear me repeat is: Early is on time. On time is late. And late is unacceptable.

I'm speaking of course about success in their academic and business careers, but the same thought applies to the golf game. If you arrive early, you'll play better.

Far too may rounds of golf start like this: Speeding into the lot, parking, grabbing clubs, running to the clubhouse to, seizing a cart and dashing to the first tee. From lot to first swing: five minutes flat. No stretching, no putting practice, no time to focus on golf and leave the workaday world behind.

It isn't possible to play good golf on that sort of schedule. Good golf requires relaxation, and freedom from tension. Running in at the last minute is guaranteed to create it.

To maximize your chances of success, arrive at least a half an hour early. Before heading to the clubhouse, make sure you have all the gear you need. You can create a lot of tension by having to run back to the car at the last moment for a ball mark repair tool or a towel.

In the clubhouse, take the time to talk to the pro. Find out where the pins are. On unfamiliar courses, see if there are any local tips or tricks and make notes. On a recent round, I was able to save several shots by aiming at the recommended local landmarks, such as "the red barn in the distance" instead of the more visually obvious. There may also be some local rules you need to know.

After visiting the clubhouse, take the time to stretch. If it's a morning round, you likely still are stiff from sleeping. On an afternoon round, the office chair will be the culprit. At the very least, driving your car to the course is going to create is going to create its own form of awkward kinks.

If there's time, hit a small bucket to loosen up. Don't try to fix any swing faults. Just work on getting some feel and rhythm. Next, stop at the putting green. Again, this isn't the time to fix swing faults. You're just trying to get a feel for the speed and a sense of rhythm.

But most of all, use the extra time to take a few deep breaths and mentally leave behind the world beyond the out-of-bounds stakes. Smell the grass. Feel the wind. Enjoy the scenery.

Relax.

Practice A Round Before You Play

On the practice tee, it's better to hit ten focused shots than a hundred unfocused ones. So if you arrive at the course early enough to hit a few before playing, stick to a small bucket. Don't pound balls trying to fix your swing issues in the fifteen minutes before your tee time. It's not going to happen.

Instead, imagine yourself on the first tee and go through your entire pre-shot routine: pick a target, visualize the shot, set an aiming point, check your alignment, take a practice swing -- everything you normally do before every shot. Then hit the range ball. For your second ball, imagine yourself in the fairway, ready for your second shot. Go through your entire pre-shot routine again. Mentally tick off two putts. Then imagine the second tee. Repeat as time allows.

Get yourself into the groove of playing golf, not golf swing.

Eat Sensibly

Watch the Tour Pros. You'll notice that they consume several small snacks over the course of a round -- an energy bar, a banana, a handful of nuts or an apple. They know that to play well, they have to maintain their energy levels.

You also may notice what they're typically *not* eating: candy, bagels, chips and other course convenience foods. That's because those foods are high on the "glycemic index." Composed mostly of sugars and other carbohydrates, they provide quick energy, but just as quickly cause an energy crash. The body's reaction to an infusion of sugars is to release insulin, which ultimately can make you feel tired and sluggish.

This isn't a tract on nutrition and body chemistry, but a little research will reveal a general consensus: the best snacks are higher in protein and fiber. These take longer to digest, and level out the insulin rush. That's why the pros are eating protein bars, nuts and apples.

Here's what I take on a round: a handful of salted almonds in a plastic baggie, an apple, and a bag of jerky.

Hydrate Your Body

By now, everyone recognizes the body's need to stay hydrated. Negative health effects aside, dehydration also can hurt your game. Even in the early states, dehydration can lead to light headedness and loss of concentration, physical weakness and muscle cramps. None of those are good for your game.

A point to remember: You start to experience the effects of dehydration before you start feeling really thirsty.

I've often wondered if poor play over the last several holes of a round could be attributed in part to muscle and mental exhaustion due to dehydration.

Especially when walking, I carry a 40oz stainless steel canteen. The beverage is water, usually "spiked" with a packet of sugar free sport mix.

Here's a trick I learned from a couple of the girls on the high school golf team I coached: The night before a round, I fill a quarter to half of the bottle with water and stick it in the freezer. That leaves a nice cold base of ice that will melt as the round wears on. (I also learned not to fill the entire bottle -- even though the top was open, it narrows, and the ice expanded horizontally, distorting the bottle. I had to bang it back with a hammer.)

Beer does not count as hydration. The alcohol actually will dehydrate you. Energy drinks and other high caffeine drinks also don't count for the same reason. There are, however, a wide variety of powdered water supplements that both add flavor and enhance hydration.

Don't Drink and Drive

Don't drink and drive -- either golf cart or off the tee.

A couple of the groups I play with drink far too much beer for the good of their games. As the round wears on, play gets sloppy and scores rise. Ironically, when I've pointed this out, the response is that they play better a "little buzzed."

They don't.

There also have been far too many reports lately of tipped golf carts -- some resulting in deaths. News reports rarely say, but my suspicion is that alcohol is involved in more than a few of those incidents.

I've even been paired with a few who have smoked pot during their rounds. Needless to say, this is a very bad idea.

Get Fit

You'll get no health and fitness advice here, other than to state the obvious: you'll play better if you're fit. So get some exercise, and take up a stretching and light weight lifting program.

From Tee To Green

Course strategy is a critical element in scoring well.

Develop A Plan

While there certainly is a thrill in waiting for the holes to unveil themselves on an unexplored course, you can improve your scores by developing a game plan before approaching the first tee.

The purpose of a game plan is to help manage expectations and emotions. A player with a game plan will not let mounting pressure force bad decisions. He will not compound the mistakes of one hole with angry and impulsive decisions on the next.

If the course is familiar, creating a game plan is not terribly difficult. Using a spare scorecard, mark the holes on which bogey would be a good score, and which you can reasonably expect par.

For each par 4 or par 5, note what club you will use off the tee. On the most basic of holes, think about the hole in reverse: First decide the club and distance for your shot into the green, then subtract that from the hole's total yardage to determine the needed tee shot length.

More problematic holes — doglegs or holes with fairway hazards — require you to think about distance to specific landing zones. If the card offers illustrations of the holes, mark these areas. In addition, for each green note which side is an acceptable miss. That can affect the plan for a landing zone and tee shot.

And in doing all of this, think about what the prevailing wind and known conditions will do to your game.

You can still create a game plan on unfamiliar courses, but it will take a closer analysis of the score card (which hopefully has some clear illustrations). You also might check for a yardage book in the clubhouse. I like to buy the yardage books not only for the information, but also as souvenirs.

If you have time to plan, many places offer course maps online. Newer GPS units offer preview modes.

Stick to the plan unless you run across unexpected yardages or conditions. A game plan will save strokes only if you are able stay focused. Don't let anger over a double on an easy par 3 push aside the plan for the next hole. If the original plan on the following tee was to hit a 5 wood, hit a 5 wood. Don't try to get those shots back by making a heroic drive. More often than not, it will turn out badly and you'll fall further behind.

Pay Attention To The Starter

On good golf courses, starters can be a source of much useful information. They've got the goods on pin locations, local rules, ground under repair and even strategy.

Don't just let the starter's words pass through your brain. Note on the scorecard any useful bits that he passes on.

The usefulness of pin locations is obvious, even if the thinking golfer doesn't necessarily go pin hunting. Where greens are large, the difference between a pin in front and to the rear can be an extra club's distance.

Local rules sometimes can be extremely useful. One course I play has large swaths of flowerbeds lining the holes. The local rule says any ball that rolls into the beds gets a free drop. Nice. Another says that any ball within the boundaries of a staked tree gets a drop.

Knowing that a hole contains ground under repair before teeing off is useful. You get a free drop from such ground, so aiming at such sometimes is clever.

Before teeing it up at a tough course in Maryland, the starter told us that the key was to keep the ball below the hole. Taking that advice to heart, I short clubbed myself at every opportunity, letting the ball bound up to the front, well below the hole locations. It worked, and I had a terrific round for the first time on a relatively difficult course.

Play Conservatively

The conservative play rarely is the most exciting, but for higher handicappers, it's usually the route to lower scores. While it's true that great reward sometimes lies at the end of a risky shot, it isn't true often enough. More generally, bad decisions and poor shots compound, and a sure bogey turns into a round destroying triple.

So leave the swashbuckling to Phil Mickelson and play for the sure thing.

Sometimes the decision is obvious. One recurring situation has a player with his ball behind a tree line and two clear choices: take a risk and try to advance the ball through a narrow gap, or choose the safer chip sideways (or even backwards) through a larger opening. Playing the safer chip absolutely will add a shot to the total, but it also will eliminate the possibility of hitting a tree and bouncing the ball further into the woods, ballooning the score.

Another is the ball-in-a-steep-bunker scenario. Playing it forward to the green is possible, but risks clipping the top and forcing the same play over (and over, and over). A choice that could ultimately result in a lower score would be to play back out of the less steep front, and then forward to the green.

Other situations are less obvious, and thus more problematic. Fairway shots to an open green often defy analysis. If all options seem equal, choose the play that makes the ensuing shot less risky.

Around the green, a friend of mine has a few rules for conservative play: "Never chip when you can putt. Never pitch when you can chip. Never take a full swing when you can pitch." Given an open path to the hole, he will putt the ball to the green from as far away as 40 yards.

Playing conservatively is tough, though. It requires a great deal of mental discipline and the ability to shrug off your partners questioning your manhood.

Think Bogey Golf

Weekenders -- and especially those who struggle to reach the low 90s (that is, the vast majority of golfers) -- should think about playing bogey golf. Playing each hole at one over par brings you to a 90 on a standard par 72. Get a par on just one of those and you'll beak 90 -- something that only 25 percent of all golfers ever legitimately accomplish.

Playing for bogey takes a lot of pressure off your game. You can play safely off the tee, instead of going for raw distance. Or you can pound the ball, knowing that you have an extra shot to chip back on to the fairway before firing at the green. Missing the green on a second shot isn't a disaster.

Bogey golf allows you to take an extra shot to reach the green, instead of risking trouble trying for regulation. Often that final shot to the green will be short enough to get you in one putt distance for a par.

Bogey golf opens enormous strategic possibilities, but doesn't necessarily consign you to an automatic one over par.

Think Rule of Five

The Rule of Five is a fresh way of thinking about the game. Simply put, the rule says to play every hole as though it were a par 5. Eighteen holes at five strokes per hole totals ninety. Do better than that on two or three holes and you'll easily get into the eighties.

As with playing for bogey, thinking in terms of the Rule of Five can take a lot of pressure off your game. You'll automatically have an extra shot on all par 4s to reach your goal. If you manage a bogey or a par on a par 3, you'll have an extra shot for one or two for one of the fives.

The pressure point in this sort of thinking is that you have to get par on the longest holes on the course. For the weekender who more often than not lacks distance, the Rule of Five can be tricky.

Play Away From Trouble

A sure way to get your score down is to avoid the disastrous holes — and that means avoiding trouble altogether.

On every hole, on every shot, take a second to identify the worst potential trouble, and then plan your shot accordingly. It's not just about where you want the ball to go on a perfectly played shot; just as important is where the ball MIGHT go if you miss.

Pick a target that lets you play away from the trouble. Taking an extra shot to avoid a hazard is better than landing in one and potentially wasting several more to get out. "No guts, no glory" is for people who don't want to break 90 consistently, let alone 80.

Bunkers and water are obvious dangers. But so are branches, side hill lies, and deep rough. Sometimes the danger is just a shot you would prefer not to make. I hate 60-yard three quarter wedges, so I consider that range a danger area.

Hazards are all relative. Chancing a bunker by playing left is better than bringing water into play on the right. If bunkers are well groomed and consistent, it may even be preferable - in some situations - to be in one. At one local par 3, there's a hole where I aim right at the greenside bunker. If I miss the green, I want to be in that bunker. A miss anywhere else results in a ball buried on a slope in deep, wedge-swallowing rough.

If there's no obvious danger on the shot you're making, think about the danger you may be setting up for the next. While there's absolutely no chance that you'll reach the bunker to the right of the green, landing on that side makes it necessary on the next swing to play over a hazard that could catch your ball and force extra shots. Avoid this by playing to the left, where the fairway runs to the green.

As is the case with most of these tips, though, you need to maintain discipline—something that even the pros have a hard time doing. In the 2010 PGA Championship, broadcaster Johnny Miller criticized Bubba Watson for choosing to play a huge looping shot designed to bring his ball in over a hazard to the green. Watson failed to execute and the ball landed in the hazard, costing him an extra shot and ultimately the championship. Miller pointed out that if Watson had played ten yards less fade, the hazard would not have come into play, reducing the damage of a shot poorly played under pressure.

Play Long When Facing Water Or Another Hazard

Golf humorist Henry Beard wrote:, "When your shot has to carry over a water hazard, you can either hit one more club or two more balls."

Truer words have never been written. Whenever you need to carry water, take an extra club. The only real downside to this strategy is in possibly missing the green long. But when you consider all the possible outcomes, that is not so bad.

If you club up, the two possible outcomes are: 1) The ball is short and hits the green or; 2) The ball misses long. In this second instance, you still have the possibility of saving par by chipping or pitching it back near the hole for a one-putt.

On the other hand, if you don't club up, there are really just two outcomes: 1) The ball hits the green or; 2) The ball comes up short and lands in the water. In the latter case, you take a penalty stroke, drop another ball and take another shot at the green, hoping to hole out for par.

Play A Long Par 4 Like A Par 5

For short and medium length hitters , getting to the green in regulation on a long par 4 requires two heroic shots. Fail to precisely nail either one and the best case scenario is that you need an extra shot to reach the green. But because longer shots magnify mistakes, you could waste a lot more trying to extricate yourself from trouble.

The solution is to play a long par 4 like a par 5. Start off the tee with a medium wood or iron that keeps you in the fairway. Hit another medium length shot following that. Having avoided trouble, your third shot should be short enough to get close to the hole. Then, you'll have a reasonable chance at par -- or bogey at worse.

Consider Playing A Strong Dogleg As A Par 5

On a dogleg four that requires a heroic tee shot to clear the corner, consider playing three shots from the fairway. Hit the ball safely to the outside line on the tee shot, clear the corner with the second and then go for the green with the third on what is likely a short- to mid-range shot. With that strategy, you've still got a chance for a single putt and a par, or at worse a bogey.

Trying to make the heroic shot around the bend brings a double or even triple into play. If you fall short on the inside line (heroic shots rarely are the accurate ones), at best you'll need an extra shot to get to the corner, and still have a long play to the green. If that heroic shot gets you off the fairway into the rough or trees, the penalty will be even more severe.

Lay Up On Long Par 3s

If a Par 3 is an uncomfortable length, lay up. Swinging hard to reach a distant green -- and especially a well-guarded one -- can run a weekender into shot wasting trouble: out of bounds, in a hazard, in thick rough around the green, or simply result in a mishit from trying too hard.

Even the pros run into this problem. At the 2011 PGA Championship, the world's best players were faced with a 260- yard par 3. Many of their rounds came undone when tee shots dropped into the water fronting the green. Interestingly, though, there's room for bailing out on the left. Playing short and left would give these pros -- who are uncannily accurate with their wedges -- a chance to hole out, or get a one putt for par.

Far better to lay up with a familiar iron, then play a pitch or lob to the green. That'll take the disastrous shot out of the equation and give you a chance at a one-putt par.

Aim For The Fat Part Of The Green On Par 3s

On a Par 3, the principal defense of the hole generally lies not in the distance, but in the bunker complexes and greens. On a well-designed course, these simplest of holes are traps for the unwary, in some ways more difficult than par 5s. And when the pins are tucked away, they are little more than lures on a hook.

The safest move for the weekender, then, is to always aim at the largest, safest part of the green. From any part of the green, a decent putter is just two strokes from the hole and par.

Think About The Third Shot On Par 5s

In planning for a Par 5, think about the third shot. Identify a distance that gives you a reasonable chance to hit the green. Subtract that from the hole's length and you'll have an idea about how far you need to hit a shot from the tee.

Let's say that the challenge ahead is a 495-yard par 5 and that your most reasonable chance to hit the green is from 110 with a 9 iron. That means that your first two shots need to cover 385 yards.

There are a lot of different ways to approach this. Two 193-yard shots (5 woods, perhaps) cover the distance, as would a 230-yard drive and a 155-yard iron. What you do depends upon your confidence and distance with the various clubs in your bag. The important thing is to get that last shot in position for your favored club.

Give Yourself Room For Error

Give yourself plenty of room for error. Sure, if you hit the perfect shot, you can clear that tree with a 9 iron. But you might be much more likely to do it with a gap wedge. It won't go as far on the other side, but you won't lose a shot when the ball comes ricocheting back at you.

Giving yourself a wide margin for error may cost you a shot. Missing on the other hand -- however narrowly --could cost you two or more.

On Every Shot

There are some things that you need to do on every shot to ensure success. Make these things a part of your playing routine and your scores will quickly go down.

Play Golf, Not Golf Swing

Don't think too much about technique on the course. Filling your head with all the swing tips you've learned from golf magazines, instruction books and videos will simply cause mental and physical confusion. The course also is not the place to start a detailed analysis of your swing.

Avoid "paralysis by analysis." Don't concentrate on the details of your swing. Instead, focus on the course and the shot, imagining what you want the ball to do, then let your swing happen.

Three things you can -- and should -- think about on the course: grip, stance and alignment. But all of those occur before the swing itself.

Remember That You Don't Need A Perfect Swing

You don't need a perfect swing -- just a consistent, repeatable one.

Anyone who's played golf for any length of time has seen players who are ruthlessly efficient with ugly swings. They aim 50 yards to the left to compensate for slices; they have a Jim Furyk hitch; chicken wings; a follow-through that spins them around; or are constantly off balance. But somehow these players manage to get around the course in a workmanlike manner.

A guy in our golf league has a double pump at the top of his swing that's so weird I try not to look for fear it's infectious. But somehow he's always at the top of the league standings. It's nasty, but it works for him.

The key here is "repeatable." Find the grip, stance, ball position and stroke that produce similar results every time. It's better to find a swing that allows you to consistently hit the 6 iron 140 yards than the one that occasionally sends the ball 160, but also may go some other unpredictable distance or direction. In the latter case, it'll be impossible for you to plan a shot.

Always remember that the game is about getting the ball into the hole with the least number of strokes. There's no bonus for having a beautiful swing.

Work On Your Alignment

If the ball is not properly aimed, you cannot possibly hit the target. Incorrect alignment also can cause horrific swing faults as your body unconsciously tries to compensate by bringing the club off plane to send the ball in the right direction.

A hallmark of the inconsistent player is that he aligns his body, rather than the ball, to the target. In reality, a player's body should be aligned to the left of the target (for a right handed golfer). That's because player and ball are on parallel lines, with the player's feet positioned to the left of the ball.

It is a mantra of golf instructors that players should imagine a railroad track, with the player standing on one rail, and the ball sitting on the other. The rail with the ball is the one that runs to the target.

Improper alignment is a mental mistake that can easily be corrected by consistently applying a preshot aiming routine.

Before taking your stance, stand behind the ball and visualize a line through the ball to the target. Keeping that line in your imagination, pick an intermediate target on the line about a foot in front of the ball. The target can be a dirt spot, a tuft of grass, a shadow or some other point.

When you step up to the ball to take your stance, align the clubface so that it is on the line running from the ball to your intermediate point. Then, take your stance, maintaining the clubface on that line. Finally, ensure that your feet and shoulders are parallel to the line created by clubface, ball and aiming point.

With the line of your body and your aiming line in parallel, take your waggle and swing away.

If your alignment has been at all out of whack, you should notice immediate improvement.

Use An Alignment Aid

Rule 8-2 actually allows you to use an alignment aid anywhere except on the green. The catch is that you must remove the aid before taking your swing.

Still, this can be useful. Set a club down and align it to the target. Then take your stance, and look down the fairway to see where your feet, shoulders and eyes align. After removing the alignment tool, be sure to align your body to the previously discovered line.

Pick A Target

On every shot, be certain to pick a target. If you do not have a target, you can be absolutely sure that you will not hit it. Failing to aim at a specific location no doubt explains why — even on the widest fairways, and with the largest of greens — so many amateurs spray the ball wildly.

I once read a story in which Ben Hogan asked a caddy where he should aim on his tee shot. The caddy pointed out a couple of trees in the distance. "Aim for those trees," the caddy advised. "Which one?" the Hawk asked.

Hogan knew that aiming in a general direction, rather than at a precise target, was asking for trouble. I'm surprised he didn't ask "which branch." The Hawk was nothing if not precise.

Imitate Hogan by choosing a precise target on every shot. Don't just aim "at the middle of the fairway" or "at the green."

For full tee shots, pick a spot in the fairway defined by a shadow, or an off-colored patch of grass. Then pick a smaller portion of that area. Divide again if possible. That's your target.

On approach shots, don't automatically choose the flag as your target. If you actually land the ball on target, it's going to release and roll to the back of the green away from the flag. And too often, the flag is in a sucker position.

Pay close attention to the next televised PGA Tour event. Notice how often the players land the ball in a spot away from the hole, only to have it roll to within inches. It's no accident. They were aiming for that precise spot, knowing where it will roll from there.

Just as with a shot from the tee box, on approach shots, you should choose as narrowly defined a target as possible. Pick a ball mark if possible; otherwise, focus on a spot and burn its location into your brain.

Picking a target is just as important around the green as it is from the tee box or fairway. It's also a easier because you're a lot closer. Aim for a dent, or even a recognizable blade of grass at the location where you want the ball to land and begin its roll toward the hole.

Having a precise target helps your game on several levels. First, it's necessary for proper alignment. You need to set up with your clubface on a line with the target, and your feet and shoulders parallel to that. None of that is possible without a precise target.

Second, having a precise target forces you to think about your goal. You're not just chunking the ball down the course. You want to place each shot with an eye to the one after that. It's not enough to land your tee shot somewhere in the fairway. You want it on the fairway in a position that maximizes your chances on the next swing.

And finally, on a more metaphysical level, focusing on a precise location allows your subconscious to come into play. Your body will try to do what the brain wants.

Aim High When Facing A Hazard

When faced with a long carry over a hazard, stop focusing on the ground, and instead pick a target line using a point well above the fairway such as a distant tree, or the top of the visible flagstick. This takes the hazard out of your line of vision, forcing you to think of something other than the water (or brush). Thinking about the hazard—even thinking you've got to get over it—makes it much more likely that you'll lose a ball.

Visualize Your Shots

I don't have a lot of use for the eastern mysticism that has pervaded the game since "Golf In the Kingdom." But I do think that the habit of visualizing a shot before taking a swing has improved my game immensely. Fixing a picture of the shot in the mind helps to reduce any possible miscommunication between eyes, brain and muscles.

It's a technique used by all great players. Jack Nicklaus wrote, "I never hit a shot, not even in practice, without having a very sharp, in-focus picture of it in my head. First I see the ball where I want it to finish, nice and white and sitting up high on the bright green grass. Then the scene quickly changes, and I see the ball going there; its path, trajectory, and shape, even its behavior on landing. Then there is a sort of fade-out, and the next scene shows me making the kind of swing that will turn the previous images into reality."

Sam Snead — in his country way — said that he would paint a picture in the sky. Tiger Woods clearly uses the technique. Watch him sometime as he stands behind the ball. He's imagining where it will go, and how it will get there.

Before every shot, I stand behind the ball and do three things. I pick a target, pick a point for alignment a few inches in front of the ball, and visualize the shot.

In visualizing the shot, I try to picture just how the ball will fly through the air (or scoot along the ground). I actually try to picture the ball as it moves in flight, capturing in my imagination the height, shot shape, landing spot and roll. I occasionally will even run through a couple of quick scenarios, as I realize that my first imaginary shot might hit an overhanging branch, or roll into a bunker.

It's important to be realistic about the results. I'm not a long hitter, so no amount of visualization is going to produce a 300-yard drive. Imagining things that can't be done will just screw up the results. And visualization is not going to fix a fundamentally bad swing.

Only once I have the shot fixed do I step up and take a swing. Of course, it doesn't always work out as planned. But having a clear goal in mind, and eliminating doubt as to what you want to do will go a long way toward maximizing the swing you have.

Ben Hogan said it best: "Don't ever hit a shot without thinking it through."

Focus On The Target, And Not The Hazard

You're going to hit what's uppermost in your mind, so focus on the target, not the hazard.

It's easier said than done, especially when a pond or marsh is between you and the fairway, or guarding the front of a green. But you've got to develop a narrow focus on your target, eliminating everything else from your mind.

There were some great scenes in the movie "The Greatest Game," where Francis Ouimet's focus was illustrated with the camera lens zooming in on the target, making it preternaturally large. That's the kind of focus you need.

Standing behind the ball, visualize it flying, landing and rolling to your target. If necessary, use your hands to create blinders blocking out the hazards as you stare down the line.

Stay Focused On Every Shot

Arriving at the course alone, as usual, I was paired with a father-son duo, both of whom were very good players. On nine, the son, playing from the back tees, hit a 300+ yard drive, pitched a shot to the center of the green, putted to within a foot -- and then missed the next putt. He missed the three foot comebacker, too.

"That's the thing about golf," his father said. "The one footers count for as much as the 300-yard drive."

That's good advice. Don't let your concentration waiver. Every stroke adds one to the scorecard.

If you find your mind wandering -- or thinking ahead to the next shot -- as you set up, that's the time to step back. Refocus on the target and then try again.

Think Ahead

Play golf as you would play chess. Better chess players think two, three, and four moves ahead, assessing every possibility and then evaluating the permutations. No one would ever play chess like most weekenders play golf -- moving a piece in the general direction of the opponent, and hoping for the best.

Before deciding on a shot, consider every possibility and permutation: "If I hit to location A, what will I have for the next shot?" And, "Will that be a better or worse shot than if I hit to location B?"

Ben Hogan said, "Placing the ball in the right position for the next shot is eighty percent of winning golf;" and "The most important shot in golf is the next one."

Billy Casper concurred. "Think ahead. Golf is a next shot game," he said. "Play every shot so that the next one is the easiest you can give yourself."

Commit To Your Shot

In golf, as in so many things, indecision is a killer. Once you've decided on a shot, commit to it wholly. If you can't commit completely, chances are it's not the right shot.

Failure to commit causes your brain to send mixed signals to your body. If you're thinking about two target lines, your body won't know which one to work on. If you can't decide whether to hit it hard or soft, you won't do either effectively.

If you find yourself in a state of indecision when setting up, step back and refocus. See if Plan B looks any better at that point.

Two time Masters Winner Bernhard Langer once said, "Be decisive. A wrong decision is generally less disastrous than indecision."

Accentuate The Positive

After assessing the situation and picking your shot, focus entirely on the positive aspects of the situation. Imagine how the shot will launch, the shape of the flight and its landing. Clear from your mind any thoughts of the out of bounds stakes, the fairway trap or the water hazard. Letting them come into play in your mind will make them more likely to come into play in your swing.

Billy Casper said, "Try to think where you want to put the ball, not where you don't want it to go."

Play Quickly

I used to tell my high school golf teams that there are two felony offenses in golf: being a slow player, and being a bad player. The key is not to commit both offenses at once. People will forgive a slow player if he's hitting greens in regulation and sinking birdie putts. And they'll forgive a bad player if he keeps the ball moving along.

Most weekenders aren't hitting greens in regulation and sinking birdie putts.

Playing quickly accomplishes more than speeding up a five-hour round. From observation of my golf teams and personal experience, I remain convinced that playing more quickly leads to better scores. All of those extra waggles, practice swings and whatnot serve only to break rhythm and clutter up the mind with swing thoughts and doubts. Far too often slower players are the victims of paralysis by analysis.

PGA Tour pros aren't doing amateurs any favors, either. Far from being an example to emulate, the pro's laborious pace of play is a trap for weekenders. And sometimes, it's a trap for the pros themselves. Sergio Garcia's game famously suffered a precipitous decline when he started gripping, regripping and waggling twenty and thirty times on each shot. Tiger Woods has been observed to deliberately slow down the pace of play to gain an advantage over a competitor who is closing in.

Playing quickly does not, however, mean that you should rush. It isn't about speeding up your swing. And playing quickly does not require that you play carelessly. The secret is to play purposefully, with focus.

Playing quickly means being prepared to take your shot as soon as it's your turn. Check your yardages and select your club while others are playing. At the same time, find your line and go through your pre-shot visualization routine. Then, when it's your turn, take a practice swing, step up to the ball, align and go. Moving quickly through a short routine will prevent all sorts of contradictory and unhelpful thoughts from leaking into your brain. Get into a playing rhythm and stay there.

Practice swings should be limited to just one. If you routinely take more, you'll fall into the trap of playing "golf swing," and not "golf." The course is not the place for working out swing flaws. Play with the swing you have that day and work out your issues on the range.

A friend of mine is notorious in the golf league for his slow play. Jeff's first practice swing never "feels right." So he makes an adjustment, and that doesn't "feel right." Then there's another adjustment, and another practice swing; and another adjustment and another swing. Finally, he declares "that was a good one" and steps up to the plate. He fiddles with his alignment, stance and grip, pumping his knees and waggling his club until finally it feels right, and unleashes a mighty blow — typically to little good effect. What's particularly funny about this sequence of events is that any knowledgeable golfer would observe that Jeff's first swing typically is his best. It's almost as if each successive practice and adjustment takes him further from the ideal.

There are a lot of Jeffs out there on the tee boxes and in the fairways.

Nowhere, though, does paralysis by analysis hit more golfers than on the greens. Following the lead of the Tour players, weekenders get into catcher's crouches, Spiderman crawls, plumb-bob, stalk the hole, and generally agonize endlessly over the putt. And all the while, contradictory swing thoughts and doubts begin to seep into their brains. And how many have you seen that, having made an analysis worthy of a quantum physicist can't get themselves to pull the trigger?

I wonder as I watch yet another plumb bobber misses a short stroke: How is it that an eight year old can complete a pass to a moving receiver without thinking, and yet an adult golfer after looking at all the angles, analyzing the break and grain and practicing stoke after stroke can still miss a three-foot putt?

I once heard a television golf analyst talk about a young golfer who was having a particularly good week putting. "He's absolutely fearless," the announcer said. "He just steps up and putts. He knows the ball is going in the hole."

No endless deliberations, just take a look at the line, and make the stroke. It's like throwing a ball into a catcher's mitt. You don't think. You just do.

One last bit of advice that teachers offer to students taking multiple choice quizzes — and yet is relevant to golf. On every question, eliminate the ridiculous choice and then go with your first instinct. Don't agonize over the choices. If you read wrong answers enough times, they will soon seem plausible.

Think about it.

Turn Off The Cell Phone

It's a problem that only a modern golfer could have: being bombarded by messages from the outside world while playing a game that requires focus, peace of mind and calm.

Turn off the cell phone and leave it in your bag. Or better yet, leave it in your car.

A lot has been written about the impropriety of phones on the course, and of the danger of having one go off while you're in the middle of a swing. But I don't think that's the primary problem. I think the primary evil of cell phones on the course lies in informational distraction. The mere presence of the things and their incoming messages takes your mind away from golf.

I've ignored my own advice far too often. I'll forget to switch the Blackberry to silent, and it will ding its new message notification. Then I wonder whether it's junk email or important. Perhaps it's a text message from my wife. Wondering distracts me from my game. So I check the message. Usually, it's junk. But often enough, it's something I need to attend to, so I begin thinking about that instead of the game. And by that point, I'm into a golfing death spiral.

Abandoning the Blackberry in my car is not really an option for me these days, since it also serves as my golf GPS. I just need to remember to switch it to the "all notifications off" mode.

Walk If Possible

Unless you are physically hampered, I think a strong argument can be made that you will play better golf when walking.

Aside from anecdotal evidence — every golfer in my circle of friends insists they play better on the hoof — there's also scientific proof: A 2008 study by the Rose Center for Health and Sports Sciences in Denver found that players scored best when using push carts or playing with a caddie. Nine hole averages in the study averaged 40 with a push cart, 42 with a caddie, and 43 when riding.

That's a six stroke difference over 18 holes. Here's the potential: if you're consistently shooting mid-90s when riding, you could regularly score in the 80s while walking.

I've got a number of unproven theories about why walking encourages better play. First, the constant physical activity — stretching the legs, swinging the arms and breathing deeply — will help to keep the muscles warm and loose. That's just the prescription for better golf.

Second, a walking regimen can put you on the way to weight loss and physical fitness. Take a look at the best players the world right now. It's not your father's PGA Tour. Fitness is a part of nearly every player's winning strategy. Walking eighteen holes over four hours can burn up to 1,800 calories and is the equivalent of 45 minutes of aerobics. Do that a couple times a week and you'll be well on your way to turning things around.

Walking keeps you in the flow of the game. While walking, you move smoothly from shot to shot, taking in the distances as you go. There's time to shake off the last shot, and start planning for the next. I count down club distances as I approach the ball to keep myself focused. 200 yards, 3 wood, 5 wood, seven 7 wood, 6 iron, 5 ... right down to where I arrive at the ball.

The cart, on the other hand — especially with a partner — is a series of disconnected stops and starts, with the distraction of another player's shots in between. In a cart, you can never get a true feel for the course's distances.

Walking gives you a lot of information about course conditions that you'll never glean whizzing about in a cart. You'll feel the direction and strength of the breezes. Your feet will sense the conditions — not only hard and soft, but also how it changes across the holes. That kind of information is invaluable and you can't get it in a cart.

Then there's the less logical. I've got this rather mystical idea that walking keeps me "connected" to the land. I just have a better feel for a course on foot. And I am a lot happier when I can take the time to drink in the sunshine, breezes and scenery.

Of course, there's a final caveat to all of this. If you're hopelessly out of shape, walking at first could actually hurt your game. When you cross your personal anaerobic threshold, the buildup of lactic acid will make your muscles burn and cause a deterioration of the fine muscle skills. That's a recipe for bad swings and the yips.

So if you haven't been walking, build up to it. Try walking three holes while your partner drives. Then six, then nine. You'll be cruising through eighteen before you know it.

Don't Play Shots You Haven't Practiced

A sure way to get into trouble on the course is to attempt a shot you haven't practiced. The pros may make the creative shots look easy, but that's just one of the many reasons they're on tour and you're not.

It's nearly always best to stick to the shots you know how to make. In some cases that means you'll have to take an indirect or even unconventional route to the hole.

If you're close to the face of a steep greenside bunker and you haven't regularly practiced the high lob sand shot, fall back to the shots you know. Play sideways or backwards to a less steep side, and move forward from there. Trying to get a ball up and over is likely to cost you several shots with no gain.

Chipping and pitching are two shots I've practiced enough to count as a strength. The flop simply is not in my repertoire. So even when faced with a situation that calls for a flop, I look for ways to pitch or chip instead. While a flop sometimes is the most direct route to the hole, for me, it's just as likely to run up the score.

In the long run, the real solution is to spend time practicing a variety of shots. When you go the range and practice areas, don't just hit the same driver and full iron shots time and again. Work on a variety of shots that you may need on the course.

Find Your "Choke Stroke"

Jimmy Demaret had in his repertoire what he called a "choke stoke" — a club that he could depend upon when nothing else was working. I think Demaret had the right idea, but the wrong name. It's not a "choke" club, but a "clutch" club, and finding it can help you salvage a round.

When the wheels come completely off my game, I turn to the 7 iron. For whatever reason — and it's probably psychological — the seven never seems to let me down. In moments of golfing crisis, I turn to the seven as a drowning man seizes a life preserver. I'll play it off the tee, out of the fairway, and as my chipping and pitching tool. Only when I feel that my groove has returned do I turn back to the rest of the bag.

You probably already have a favorite club in your bag. The next time nothing else seems to be working, find a way to use that stick — even if it seems somehow inappropriate to the job.

If the driver's not working, and you resort to your favorite 6 iron off the tee, it'll likely take you an extra shot to reach the green. But at least you won't be hitting three from the tee after yanking one out of bounds. And if you're well inside the 6 iron's range to the green, choke up or take a three quarter swing. But get that club into your hands until your problems work themselves out.

Waggle The Club -- Just A Little

Tension is the enemy of the golf swing. Incorporating a bit of a waggle into your preshot routine can help ease that tightness.

But don't overdo it. Too much waggle distracts from the job at hand. It becomes an excuse to not hit the ball; a habit that becomes its own end. It's sort of the full-swing's version of putting paralysis.

Worse, it makes you look like an idiot.

Adjust for Elevation

When facing an uphill or downhill shot, you need to adjust your club selection. Assuming that you know your regular distances, the rule of thumb is to add or subtract one club for each ten yards of elevation.

A second consideration: On severe uphill shots, make sure the club has enough loft to clear the sides of the hill. You may correctly judge distance, but a low flying ball that slams into a steep uphill slope can put you in an awkward spot. In that case, laying up may be in order.

There's a short par 4 at a local course that — were it flat — would easily be reachable for many with a 5 wood or long iron. The green, however, sits on a plateau some 30 yards above the fairway. Worse, the sides of the slope are nearly vertical and covered with knee high weeds. In this case, taking an additional club make no sense whatsoever. You'll get the distance, but the shot won't have the height to clear the hill. For most, a driver would simply result in the ball bounding into that ball-swallowing, impossibly steep slope.

Conversely, on downhill shots, make sure that you don't generate too much loft. A shot sailing downhill will result in additional carry and roll, but also create the effect of additional loft, with the ball plummeting straight of the sky and stopping quickly. On steep downhill shots, a three quarters shot with a lower lofted club may be in order.

Adjust For Wind

The general rule for dealing with breezes is to add or subtract one club for each 10 mph of wind. The trick is knowing just how fast the wind is blowing. The Beaufort Wind speed scale can give you an idea of wind speed:

- At 4 - 7 mph, you'll feel the wind on your skin. Leaves rustle in the trees, and weather vanes begin to move. This is pleasant golf.
- At 8 - 12 mph, you'll notice leaves and small twigs in constant motion. Flags on the sticks will begin to extend.
- At 13 - 17 mph, dust and loose paper will begin to blow around. Small branches in the trees will move. You will notice your ball going off line.
- At 18 - 24 mph, branches of a moderate size will move. Small trees begin to sway. Your ball threatens to move on the green.

- At 25 - 30 mph, large branches will sway. Umbrella use becomes difficult (and if you're in the rain with 30 mph wind, you probably shouldn't be on the course anyway).
- At 31 - 38 mph, whole trees are in motion. Effort is needed to walk against the wind. Head for the clubhouse. Stay away from trees.
- Anything Faster: Get off the course immediately.

So, with twigs and small branches moving, add one club. If larger branches are swaying add two.

It is important to notice not only how things are on the ground, but also what's happening up in the air. On tree lined fairways, there are dead zones where the wind is screened. High golf shots, however, get caught up in the breezes. While assessing the situation, notice how the wind affects the upper branches.

Hitting the ball harder into the wind isn't a solution. A harder shot will increase the spin and exaggerate the wind conditions. Take more club.

Estimating what to do in a crosswind is tricky. In a crosswind, your ball will not only lose distance (though likely not as much as directly into the wind), but also drift in the direction it's blowing.

If you've got the game, you can try to spin the ball into the wind to hold the line. For most of us, though, the solution is to try to compensate for the drift by aiming more left or right. A rule of thumb is to aim five yards left or right for every ten mph of wind speed.

Crosswinds exaggerate your ball's natural flight. If you're a slicer, a wind blowing to the right will carry your ball right off the course. Remember to compensate for that, also.

This all creates some very interesting calculus as you're not only trying to figure how much club, but also how far left and right.

A final solution—again, if you've got the game—is to hit a punch shot, keeping the ball on a boring trajectory under the wind.

Watch Your Grip Tension

Advice on the golf grip ranges from holding the club like a baby bird (Sam Snead) to gripping it relatively tight; most teachers seem to tell their students to hold the club in the fingers, but there's a significant school of thought that focuses on the palm. Strong grip. Weak grip. Choke down. Finger on top. Vardon. Overlapping. Baseball. The variety seems endless.

Whatever program you subscribe to, though, you should be aware of how the tension in your grip changes over the course of the round. Under pressure, the natural inclination is to clamp down and grip every more tightly. If you start out light, it'll be tight; start out firm, and you'll end up with a death grip. Either way, the results won't be good.

Make a mental note to specifically check your grip pressure several times during a round -- and especially before a pressure shot.

Inspect Your Divots

If you need a mid-round check on your swing, inspect your divots. The direction of the divots will tell you where your clubface is going. The depth will tell you a lot about how steep or shallow you're coming into the ball. If you can remember where the ball was located, the divot also can tell you how far behind the ball you're striking.

Make adjustments accordingly.

Watch Where Your Ball Goes

A lost ball will cost you stroke and distance, so pay attention to where it goes. As soon as you have a bead on the ball's landing spot, pick out a landmark on that line. Then, when you get out into the fairway (or sadly, the rough), you can position yourself between the landmark and the tee box to help locate the ball.

Control. Your. Anger.

Getting angry at the game, your clubs, the ball, your partners, or the guys in front of you does absolutely no good. Anger leads to tension, and tension will cost you strokes. Anger causes loss of focus, and loss of focus will cost strokes.

Tommy Bolt, who was inducted into the Hall of Fame in 2002, was famous for his outbursts of anger, which often resulted in clubs soaring through the sky. "Always throw clubs ahead of you," he quipped. "That way you won't waste any energy going back to pick them up." He also advised players "Never break your driver and your putter in the same round."

Terrible Tommy won fifteen times on the PGA Tour, but Ben Hogan said, "If we could've screwed another head on his shoulders, Tommy Bolt could have been the greatest who ever played."

Anger issues in golf generally stem from making bad shots -- or even a series of them. The general advice on dealing with anger is to count to ten, or to take long, deep breaths. I had a hippie teacher who once told the class that to get rid of our anger we should imagine blowing our troubles into a balloon and then letting it drift upward into a cloudless sky.

But here's some more golf-specific advice:

First, if you're in a cart, get out and walk; let your partner drive. Take a likely club with you and swing it to let out some tension. Along the way, avoid dwelling on the previous bad shot by thinking obsessively about the next. As you approach the ball, speculate on the next target, the distance, the lie, the wind and the club you'll need. Play out several next shot scenarios in your head. That sort of cold analysis will help you to quickly get over the emotions associated with the last shot.

On The Tee

Lower scores begin with a smart tee shot on every hole.

Abandon The Driver

For players without the mad recovery skills of a Woods or Mickelson, a big key to scoring low is keeping the ball in the fairway. Using the 3 wood off the tee is a strategy more weekenders should employ.

Over the years, studies have shown that the average golfer hits a 3 wood just as far -- if not further -- than the driver. That, combined with the greater accuracy of a club with a shorter shaft and higher loft makes the 3 wood a perfect club off the tee. Even if you were to give up ten yards, the greater probability of hitting the fairway still generally makes the 3 wood a better play.

Giving up the driver is tough, though. We've been conditioned by both the pros and advertising to believe that the driver is the proper tool for the tee box. The best thing to do is to go cold turkey and just leave it in your trunk.

Occasionally, as an exercise with the high school golf teams I coached, I would confiscate their drivers for a practice round. It caused a great deal of consternation at first, but made them realize that there are many ways to play a golf hole -- and some smarter than others.

Jerry Barber said, "The woods are full of long hitters."

Play From The Correct Tees

One of the reasons scores are so high -- and rounds so long -- is that too many weekenders play from the wrong tees. Playing from the back tees might be manly, but often makes little sense. If you have to consistently make heroic drives to have a decent chance at greens in regulation, or if you find yourself playing long irons and woods into every par 4, chances are the course is too long from those tees.

Forcing yourself to hit those extra yards causes more missed fairways. Drives that fall too far from the green force the use of long irons and fairway woods. That results in missed greens, piling up strokes with costly chips, flubbed flops and multiple shots out of greenside bunkers. Long shots into the green leave players far from the hole, requiring extra putts.

One rule of thumb is to play from the tees that give you a decent chance at using a mid or short iron on the par 4s. That requires that you have a realistic understanding of how far you hit your clubs.

If your typical driver shot is 220 yards, and your 6 iron goes 170, then on a par 4, you should play from the tees that are closest to 390 from the green.

Another way to assess the proper length is to use the Rule of 28, as described by Chris Mile, owner of the Miles of Golf pro shop in Ypsilanti, Michigan. Mile says that to find the proper tees, you should multiply your average driving distance by 28. That'll give you the yardage that you should play from; choose the tees closest to that distance.

This means that a player who hits the ball 200 yards on a drive should play from the tees closest to 5,600 yards.

I use the 200-yard drive figure deliberately. Studies have consistently shown that the average golfer drives the ball 200 yards, but THINKS he hits it 30 yards further. And remember that it's the AVERAGE that counts. Occasionally uncorking a 270 yarder is not the same as hitting for an average of 270.

Tee Up On The Correct Side Of The Tee Box

Weekenders don't often take full advantage of the tee box. Too often, players spike the ball down in the center of the teeing area, without regard for the shape of the hole or the location of the hazards. Worse, when they do set up to one side, it's often the wrong one.

The natural inclination when presented with a hazard is to tee up as far away from the hazard as possible. Unfortunately, the natural inclination is often wrong.

To maximize the geometry of a hole, a better strategy is to tee up on the same side as the hazard. Slicers and straight hitters then can aim at an angle diagonally away from the hazard, bringing the maximum amount of fairway into play. Hookers can aim parallel to the hazard and rely on their hook to curve the ball away from the hazard back to the fairway. Either way, the geometry works for you.

More advice: On a dogleg left, tee off from the right. On a dogleg right, tee off from the left. Again, it's all about the geometry.

Finally, all other things being equal, slicers should tee up on the right side, and play diagonally to the left side of the fairway. Hookers should tee up on the left side and play across to the right. In both cases, the idea is to play the ball so that it comes back into the fairway, rather than trying to prevent it from going out.

Maximize Your Use of the Tee Box

When setting up your shot, use all of the teeing ground to your advantage. The rules permit a player to tee up anywhere between the markers, and up to two club lengths behind. And if you really want to maximize the tee box, remember that you actually can stand outside the teeing ground, so long as the ball is in it.

Take advantage of this rule to find a flat, undamaged area in which to spike your ball. In addition, make sure that you have solid footing. The two club lengths of extra space behind the line may also give you a more advantageous angle, or help to take an overhanging branch out of play.

Always Tee It Up On A Par 3

Jack Nicklaus said, "Always -- and I mean always -- tee the ball on par 3 holes or any other time you play your opening shot with an iron."

If it's good enough for Jack Nicklaus, it's good enough for weekenders.

Hit To Your Favorite Club's Distance

Off the tee (and on the second on par 5s), plan your shot so you can follow up with a favorite club from a comfortable distance.

If you are going to score well, it is not enough to simply hit the ball as far as you can. "As far as you can" often results in awkward yardage, forcing you to take a shot into the green with a club you'd rather not hit. Instead, think about your ideal shot into the green, and play a club that will get you to that yardage.

I'm in love with my 7 wood, so on long par 4s, I go with a club off the tee that will get me to the 7 wood range. On a par 5, I'll play my second shot so that I get to the 100- to 120-yard range -- distances I'm more comfortable with than inside 100.

Planning for these shots requires that you think backward on every hole. Start with the shot you want to take into the green, and then plan your tee shot to get you there.

On particularly troubling holes, consider using your favorite club from tee to green. It's a one-club strategy that I used in getting absolute beginners to score decently in competition (and occasionally win). If your best club is a seven or eight iron, even a 400 yard par 4 is in reach in three shots. At 130 yards a clip, the tee shot leaves you 270 out; the second leaves you at 140. That means your third will get you onto the front side of the green. Two putts, and you're down with a bogey.

Just Get The Ball In Play

On the first tee, concentrate on putting the ball in play. Starting with a double bogey because you nervously sliced the ball out of bounds can ruin your whole day. Falling a couple of shots "behind" at the outset puts undue pressure on you for the rest of the round.

It's also good advice for the rest of the round. If you're a weekender who hits most of his second shots from the rough, scale it back a bit on the tee and get the ball in play.

In The Fairway

If everything's gone right, your second (and your third) shot will be from the fairway. A smart play here puts you in scoring position.

Be Aware Of Hole Locations

It pays to know the location of the holes --
and it is often not enough to simply see the flag.
Elevated greens, swales, bunkers and the shape of
the green generate optical illusions (often
intentionally) that mask the hole's true location. "I
thought the flag was further back (closer, more left,
more right)" is a common line among weekenders
approaching the green.

Distances to the flag can be particularly
deceiving when using a laser range finder. A range
of 140 to a flag at the back of a green is very
different from 140 to the front

Knowing where flag is located relative to the
boundaries of the green and to the green's defenses
is critical information in planning shots. From the
tee, the flag location influences the side of the
fairway you want your shot to land. From the
fairway, that location tells you whether you should
be pin-hunting or looking for a safe place to bail
out.

As a course regular, take mental notes on flag
locations. After a couple of rounds, a quick visual
scan will tell you where the flag is located and
dictate your play. If you keep your own yardage, so
much the better.

On unfamiliar courses, ask the starter about hole locations. Many courses divide their greens into imaginary zones, and scorecard illustrations show the zone locations. Some municipal courses and lower end daily fee courses don't have such niceties, but the starter still should be able to tell you whether the flags are forward or back.

Concentrate On Hitting The Green

Among Cary Middlecoff's 41 professional victories were two U.S. Opens and a Masters. The good Doctor thus was in a position to offer a prescription for better golf when he said, "Concentrate on hitting the green. The cup will come to you."

It's really good advice. For most amateurs, the best strategy is to get the ball onto the green as quickly as possible. Once there, you can get out the flat stick and go to work. The putting stroke is the easiest to master; with just a little practice, anyone can become a good putter.

To Middlecoff's doctrine, add this corollary: Concentrate on hitting the middle of the green. Because pinpoint accuracy is not a hallmark of the mid- to high-handicapper, from the fairway it's best to aim at the biggest target: the center of the green. From that point, missing by a few yards doesn't put your ball in any further danger.

Take An Extra Club; Swing Easy

When in-between clubs, the sensible thing to do is to play the longer club and swing easy or choke up a bit. The alternative -- swinging harder with a shorter club -- just has too many downsides. Swinging harder will get you of rhythm, pull you off plane and make it more likely that you will top, chunk or otherwise mishit the ball.

Aim Correctly On Sidehill Lies

Sidehill lies change the angle of your swing, and thus your ball flight, so plan accordingly.

When the ball is below your feet, your swing tends to get more steep, and creates a left to right spin on impact. Compensate by aiming slightly left and playing a fade to bring the ball back to its target.

When the ball is above your feet, your swing tends to get flatter, creating a right to left spin. The way to compensate for this is to aim further right and allow the draw to bring it back to the proper line.

Compensate For An Uphill Lie

The uphill lie requires planning to play effectively. The most important thing is to align your body with the slope of the ground. This allows your swing to follow the slope down and then back up.

Second, in aiming, you need to compensate for the fact that your altered stance will tend to push the ball left.

Finally, remember that the slope will effectively increase the loft of your club. Compensate by taking more club than you usually would at that distance, and moving the ball to the center of your stance.

Compensate For A Downhill Lie

When playing on a downhill lie, know that the ball will fly lower and roll more. To correct, take a higher number club.

When setting up, align your shoulders with the slope of the ground and swing along the slope.

Don't Give Up On A Hole

It's natural to become dejected after starting a hole with a couple of bad shots. But don't give up -- that's where the extra strokes can pile up. Bear down and resolve instead to make each shot better than the last. Stay in your routine.

The great Walter Hagen once said, "Three bad shots and one good one equals par."

Where To Lay Up

Faced with the choice of attempting a heroic shot -- and possibly catastrophic shot -- or taking two safe shots, the sensible thing to do is to lay up. The question is: where?

The first rule is not to take any chances. If you are going to take risks, you may as well try that heroic shot. The goal is two safe shots.

After that, what? The ideal layup position is a flat spot where you can take a full swing with a comfortable club. You don't want your second shot to involve a three quarter wedge or a sidehill lie.

Sometimes, the layup will seem absolutely ridiculous. It doesn't matter. The goal is to save shots. A pair of pitching wedge shots to cover 200 yards makes sense if the green is fronted by water.

Off The Fairway

In spite of every precaution, the weekender still will too often land off the fairway, finding trouble in the rough, traps, hazards and trees. Handling these properly can limit the damage and keep your scores down.

Get Out Of The Rough

If you get off the fairway into deep rough, your first thought should be about minimizing the damage by getting back to the fairway. Swinging harder to make it to the green in regulation, or taking a longer club is often a recipe for disaster. You *might* overcome the bad lie, but it's just as likely you'll find yourself hitting out of the rough again on the next.

Focus instead on getting back to the fairway where you can maximize your chances of success on the next swing. Take a higher lofted club and worry only about the distance back to the fairway.

When the rough is particularly grim and the possibility of a one shot recovery slim, consider the unplayable lie. It'll cost you a stroke, but could result in a better position.

Get Out Of Jail

If, in spite of all precautions, you still end up off the fairway into the trees (we call that being "in jail" in Michigan) your first and only thought should be to get back onto the fairway. Ignore that two-foot gap between the trees 30 yards away that gives you a shot at the green. You might make it, but you also could hit an overhanging branch, or a tree trunk and end up deeper in trouble.

The prudent thing to do is to take your lumps and aim for the biggest gap you can find -- even if it means going backwards. Reversing course is preferable to losing two or more strokes ricocheting balls off the trees.

A shot you can try: use your driver or 3 wood to "putt" the ball back to the fairway. Scooting the ball along the ground takes overhanging branches out of the equation.

Get Out Of The Bunker

When caught in a fairway bunker, your top priority is to get back to the grass. The worst possible outcome is to catch the lip of the bunker and find yourself expending yet another shot trying to get out of the sand.

Abandon any thoughts of the heroic shot. Instead, take your punishment and use a higher lofted club to get the ball up in the air and back to the short grass. You'll still have a chance at bogey -- or perhaps even par -- and keep the hole from becoming a disaster.

Bobby Jones said that "too much ambition is a bad thing to have in a bunker."

Around The Green

Focus and strategy are as important around the green as from the tee box or fairway. It does absolutely no good to get close to the green in regulation and then spend several shots trying to get on.

Plan Your Greenside Shots To Assist Your Putts

The key to the one-putt is being close enough after the approach to make that a reasonable proposition. If you're consistently forty feet away from the hole when you take your stance for the first putt, you're going to have a lot of two -- and perhaps even three -- putt greens.

Get your approach shots close. And plan those shots so that the misses don't leave you with an evil putt.

If at all possible, leave your shot under the hole. Putts uphill to a hole are far easier than downhill or across the slope.

Visualize the hole is as the center of a clock face, with the twelve o'clock on the high side, and the six o'clock on the low. The ideal approach will leave the ball between four and eight. A terrible approach would leave the ball between two and four, or eight and ten.

Putt Whenever Possible

A putt is the safest play in golf. It has the fewest moving parts, and avoids the risk of blading the shot or hitting it fat. The worst putt will always be better than your worst flop, pitch or chip.

Whenever your ball is around the green, strongly consider the possibility of putting. If the grass is relatively short and the ground even, it's a no-brainer. Get out the flat stick.

When To Chip

Because a chip is made with a short, more horizontal motion, it's a good shot for poor lies, close lies and hardpan. The steeper descent of a pitch will likely cause the club to skip and send the ball soaring over the green.

A chip also is also probably your best bet on downhill shots. It'll get the ball rolling as soon as possible, helping to prevent it from getting away from you.

If your choice is a chip or a lob, always go with the chip.

When To Pitch

A pitch is made with a steeper angle than a chip, and thus is a good choice on good lies and soft ground. In those cases, you'll be able to strike down without fear of hitting it thin.

Pitching the ball also is really the only choice for an uphill target, or when it is necessary to clear an obstacle, or rough that won't allow a roll.

With just a little bit of practice, a pitch will become a reliable shot in your arsenal – one that you'll want to return to whenever feasible.

Chip With The Correct Club

A chipping stroke is easy. Picking the right chipping club is a little more complicated.

Most of my playing partners use the same club for every chip. It's out of the bag before they even have a chance to evaluate the situation. What they try to do is vary their stroke, not the club. This often leads to one of two situations: the ball is either habitually left short (often not getting out of the rough), or blown by the hole.

Vary your chipping club -- not your stroke -- according to the situation. Here's a rule of thumb: a 9 iron will fly a quarter of the way to the hole and roll the rest. A pitching wedge will fly halfway and roll halfway. A sand wedge will fly three quarters of the distance and roll one quarter.

Of course, you need to gauge you own distances and ball behavior. Just as you verify the distances on a full swing, know what happens for each of your clubs on a chip.

Try A Specialized Chipping Club

Play around the green is so important that if your short game isn't strong, you might consider a chipping club. These typically feature large, flat-bottomed heads with a steep face attached to a putter shaft. The flat bottoms allow you to get the face under the ball -- avoiding a skull -- while preventing you from digging in as the club passes through. The putter shaft offers more control by encouraging a smooth putting-style stroke.

They actually can work pretty well.

Pay Attention To the Bounce

Bounce is an indication of how much the sole of the club lifts the leading edge. A high bounce on a sand wedge is useful because it allows the club to pass through sand without digging in. Conversely, on tight lies, you need a club with less bounce to keep the leading edge from bounding into the ball, causing a "thin" hit.

Around the greens, pay attention to the ground before choosing your wedge. If the grass or sand is fluffy, choose a club with a higher bounce. When the lies are tight, or the sand hard, you're better off with less bounce.

If you're consistently sending your ball flying from one side of the green to the other, or leaving it woefully short, chances are you're using a club with the wrong bounce.

Pick A Landing Spot

Be precise. Around the green, it's not enough to just aim the ball in the direction of the hole. Whether pitching, chipping or lobbing, pick a spot on the green for the ball to land. Then, visualize how the ball will roll once it hits that spot. Visualizing how the shot will play out will help you get up and down more often.

Learn The Bump And Run

The tendency in well-watered, American parkland golf is to fly the ball to the target. However, with dry conditions, closely cut grass and/or an open front to the green, the "bump and run" often is a safer play.

Several things make the bump and run appealing. First, it's a very simple stroke. You'll master the bump and run long before you become competent with the wedges. And if you're not breaking 90, you haven't mastered the wedges.

Second, because it's so simple, the bump and run minimizes mistakes. After even a little practice, there's scant chance of a skulled ball, a fat shot or any of the other dangers a wedge presents.

Third, the bump and run makes it easy to control distances -- and in the end, it's all about controlling distance. Wedge play gets complicated and unpredictable with full, three quarters and half swings. You can use the same bump and run stroke with different clubs to get the distance you want.

And finally, the bump and run is less susceptible to the vagaries of the wind. That's why it's the play of choice in Scotland.

A bump and run isn't flashy. It won't impress your playing partners. But it gets the job done.

Pitch With a 7 or 8 Iron Into The Wind

A pitching wedge flies just high for the wind to affect distance and accuracy. A headwind can make a ball climb and cause you to lose distance. Crosswinds can blow you off the green.

When pitching into the wind, try using a seven 7 or an 8 iron. It'll keep the ball on a lower trajectory, with less spin.

Leave The Flag In

Leave the flag in for shots from off the green. Studies have shown that amateurs make more shots with the pin in than out. It's likely this is so because the flagstick will act as a backstop on shots hit too hard. The flagstick may also force you to focus more clearly on a target, rather than a generalized area around the hole.

In fact, there was a time when the rules of golf permitted the flagstick to remain in the hole when a player was putting -- as long as he was at least 20 yards away. Players could -- and did -- take advantage of that when striking a ball forcefully on a lag putt. You may have seen Arnold Palmer leave the flagstick in on a putt in replays of the 1962 Masters (or, if you are of a certain age, you may actually have seen it in person).

You can be certain that leaving the flag in the hole confers a competitive advantage because the ruling powers have made it illegal to do so from on the green

On The Green

Putting is the easiest stroke in golf -- I've never seen anyone whiff a putt. But it also may be the toughest shot mentally. Don't stop thinking just because you're a couple of feet from the hole.

Get A Putter Fitting

Clubfitting for irons and woods (metals) is critical. Just as critical is putter fitting. You won't be able to make a consistently good stroke if your putter has too much loft or too little; is too long or short, too light or heavy,

I don't think it's any coincidence that every good golfer I know (myself included) has a dozen or more putters lying around. That's because we are constantly in search of "the one."

It would have been a lot easier, cheaper and a more productive to have gotten a proper fitting in the first place.

Practice Putting

Seriously. Practice your putting. Work at it until your partners notice your smooth, beautiful putting stroke. Work on hitting it straight every time. If you miss a putt, make sure it's from a bad read, not a poor stroke.

Two shots on every hole are allocated for putting. The fastest way to lower scores is to improve your putting.

It's worth saying again: a two inch putt counts the same on a scorecard as a 300-yard drive.

Know Your Putting Distances

As a part of practice, learn your putting distances -- just as you learned how far you hit each of your irons and woods. Learn how far the ball goes with each variation of your back and through stroke.

Distance control is the key to good putting. If you miss an inch right, you don't want the ball to scoot five feet past the hole. An aiming miss can't be compounded by a distance miss.

Concentrate On Distance

While reading break is important, getting the correct distance is even more so. If you're not certain of the break -- indeed, even if you are -- make sure that you lock in on the distance.

My teaching pro friend says that on the first putt of any considerable distance, a player should aim at an imaginary two foot circle around the hole. Sometimes the ball will go in, but getting inside this circle practically guarantees you can hole the second.

Don't Leave It Short

Don't leave a putt short. Putts that stop short of the hole never fall in. Leaving it short on a green is a waste of a stroke. A foot past the hole is always better than a foot short.

No Three Putts

One of the fastest ways to lower your scores is to eliminate the three putt.

The weekender absolutely will miss the first putt more often than not. The pros don't do much better; the best putters on tour average 1.7 strokes per hole.

The key here is to ensure that your second putt is no more than a couple of feet.

Pay Attention To The Grain On The Green

A green's grain is the direction in which the grass is growing. Believe it or not, this actually has an impact on putting. A putt that goes with the grain will travel further than one against it.

There are several ways to determine the grain of a green.

The first take some sensitivity to color. If the green appears light from your stance, you're putting with the grain. If it appears dark, you're putting against it.

Another technique is to look at the grass growing over the cup. The direction of the blades will be more obvious there.

Brushing the grass in the direction of the putt can reveal information. If the grass stands up, you're going against the grain. If it lies down, you're with it. Be careful, however. Under Rule 16, it's illegal to touch the line of a putt, or test the surface of a putting green. Make sure you conduct this experiment somewhere on the fringe behind your ball.

In many cases, you'll find that the grass grows in the direction of water flow. If the slope of the green drains downward to a pond or creek, the grass probably grows in that direction also. My golfing buddies say that balls are attracted to water; in this case, it may be true.

You also might read the sun. Like all plants, grass tends to grow toward the sun. The grain will run against your shadow.

There's a story -- probably apocryphal -- about caddies who would help their players by allowing their shadow to cast across the line of the opponent's ball. This would cause the grass to stand up, slowing the ball and perhaps making it fall short or go offline.

Armed with this granular information, you can then make a more informed decision about your putt. Working against a grain, you need to putt a little harder, and plot a little less break. Working with the grain, strike it a little less and assume more break.

Pay Attention To Green Firmness

Feel the green beneath your feet. Generally speaking, hard greens are faster and balls are less affected by break. Soft, slower greens will require a more firm stroke, and balls are more affected by break.

Pick A Midpoint To Aim

If you watch Tour caddies help their players line up putts, you'll notice that they point at spots between the ball mark and the hole. Even as a player is lining up, caddies will use the end of the flag to designate a spot.

That's because the Tour players are aiming the ball straight at that spot. The speed of the ball dictates how it will curve as it approaches and then goes past that spot.

The lesson for weekenders is that you often don't aim straight at the hole. As in lining up a shot from the tee or fairway, pick an intermediate spot and aim for that point. Then, worry about the stroke and ball speed.

Read Enough Break

Read enough break into your putts. Studies have shown that amateurs consistently do not play enough break and end up with their balls on the low side of the cup. Professionals, on the other hand, tend to miss on the high side.

High is better. A putt that skirts the high side of a hole still has a chance to fall in. A putt on the low side just keeps rolling away.

Two faults likely cause this error. First, players forget that -- like irons and metals -- the line of the putt is a foot or two in front of and parallel to the body. Aiming your feet and shoulders at the hole practically guarantees that you'll miss under the hole.

Second, weekenders tend to focus on the hole. If there's break, and you're going straight at the hole, the ball will miss.

Speed Affects Break

Remember that the harder you hit the ball, the less the less breaks in the green will affect the ball. Every golfer has heard the phrase: I hit it right through the break.

Conversely, a slower putt will be more affected by the break.

The Ball Breaks More With Distance

A ball's initial speed will cause it to go straight for the first several feet. As it gets further away, however, it loses momentum and is more affected by the slopes of the green.

Plan for this when plotting the midpoint of your putt.

Adjust Break On Uphill and Downhill Putts

You're likely not hitting a downhill putt very hard, so there is less initial speed, and the ball will not hold its starting line for very long. Thus, a downhill putt is more affected by break.

Conversely, because putting a ball uphill requires more force, it will hold the line longer and play through many breaks.

Find The Fall Line On A Sidehill Putt

Sidehill putts are probably the trickiest in golf because they are both uphill and down. The first portion of a sidehill putt must be uphill, to get to the point where forward momentum falters and the ball falls downhill to the hole.

The key is deciding on the point where you want the ball to lose its forward momentum and then turn downward. Use your distance control skills to control the putt so that the ball begins to lose momentum at that point.

Pay Attention To Putting Grip Pressure

Just as grip tension affects your full swing, it also changes your putting. Under stress, or as the round unfolds, players tend to grip with ever more strength. This tension continues up your arms, to your shoulders, back and hips, destroying the smooth stroke you've grooved in practice.

The proper amount of grip strength is different for every player, but the principle is constant. Pay attention to how you're holding your grip. Waggle the putter a little to shake out the tension, or shake your hands and arms before taking your grip and stance.

There Are No Gimmies

There are no gimmies in the rules of golf.

Putt out on every hole. Some shots may look as though you can't miss -- and maybe you can't -- but if you get used to losing focus at the end of every hole, it'll cost you. There will come a time when you have a short putt that you have to make honestly, and you won't be able to execute.

Know The Rules

Take advantage of options offered by the rules to help you score.

Learn The Basics

Learn the basics of the rules of golf.

The USGA says that there are just 34 rules of golf, but that's a bit deceiving. Each of those 34 has several sub sections, and seemingly innumerable "rulings and decisions."

Even so, the average player needs not worry about a good many of these. Read over the rules of golf and make note of the ones that apply to situations you'll encounter on the course.

Three most frequently mishandled:

On balls that are hit out of bounds or lost, the penalty is stroke and distance. This means that the player must return to the spot where the ball was last hit and play again, taking a one stroke penalty.

To speed up play, if there's ever a doubt, play a provisional ball.

The second involves Rule 13, which covers improving lies, the stance, or line of play. You can't nudge a ball out of a divot. You can't break off the branches of a tree so that you have room for a swing. And you can't fix surface irregularities. Penalty: two strokes.

And finally, you can't ask an opponent for advice (nor give it) either on how to play a shot, or on club selection. However, you can ask your partner if playing a golf game involving partners.

There are others. Pay attention to them. You will never know how good you are at golf unless you play by the rules.

Play By The Rules

It is to your benefit to play by the rules whenever practical. If you get into the habit of bending and breaking when you're on your own or in playing casual rounds, you'll forget yourself when playing in a league or club competition.

That said, there are a two rules I break on a regular basis:

First, even though the Rules and Decisions say otherwise, I treat a ball in poison ivy the same as a ball sitting on a rattlesnake. In that case, I drop the ball within one club length no closer to the hole without penalty. Poison ivy may not be an issue on the closely manicured courses the rules makers play, but it's a big deal on the tracks I frequent.

And second, on leaf buried autumn fairways, a ball lost in plain sight is played without penalty from the nearest agreed upon location.

Take the Unplayable Lie

There comes a time in every round (or perhaps every couple of rounds) when the ball gets into a desperate position: deep in the branches of a bush, up against a rock, or buried under the overhanging ledge of a trap. Worse, the ball may be in a position where a swing could endanger body or clubs.

Fortunately, there's an option: the unplayable lie. It's a one stroke penalty, but is often a better choice than taking four or five shots to get out of an untenable position. And it's always a better choice than risking injury.

Under Rule 28, a player may declare a ball to be unplayable in any place but a water hazard.

Once a ball is declared unplayable, a player has a couple of options. The first is to go back and play the ball again from the original spot. The second is to drop the ball two club lengths from the unplayable position, but no closer to the hole. The final one is to move back as far as you like on a line drawn between the hole and the unplayable spot.

Any of these are better options than taking six shots to extract your ball from an impossible spot.

Know Your Options On A Hazard

When you lose your ball in a hazard, you can choose the best of several options.

First, you can drop where the ball last crossed the hazard. Most players will choose this option.

It isn't always the best, though. Areas around a hazard present their own complications: undergrowth, long grasses, overhanging branches and steep slopes. That spot also may present an awkward distance for you.

You're already taking a penalty. Why make the recovery more complicated than necessary?

A second option is to drop the ball anywhere within two club lengths from the spot where the ball last crossed the hazard, so long as it is no closer to the hole. This is often a good option, as it allows you to find a drop spot that's more favorable.

Two club lengths might not do it, though, especially if it leaves you with an awkward distance or angle. In this case, you should consider another option: returning to the previous location. If that distance and angle was comfortable for you, it makes sense to try another shot from that position.

A final option is to draw an imaginary line from the hole through the point where the ball crossed the margin, extending backward to infinity. You can drop anywhere along that line. (Note that this line is not necessarily the line from the original spot to the hole. You may have sliced it considerably, so the line would be right of the original.)

Here's how to take advantage of that rule. Suppose that you plunked your ball into a hazard fronting the green. Dropping where the ball crossed leaves 60 yards -- not a good distance for you. Returning to the spot where you hit it from isn't good either. Using the line rule, you can back up to 100 yards and hit a comfortable shot.

On a lateral hazard, a player has the option of dropping the ball within two club lengths of a spot that is the same distance from the hole, but on the opposite margin of the hazard.

With this last, imagine a hole that has a creek running its length. The ball crosses the line of the creek on the fairway side, crosses over the line on the opposite bank, and then rolls back into the creek. The point of reference is where ball last crossed the hazard -- the opposite side of the creek. This rule, however, allows a player to drop at a spot equally far from the hole, but on the fairway side.

Finally, a hole may have a drop area for balls that cross into a hazard.

The key to all of this is to use the rules of golf to choose the best location from which to drop your ball and hit your next shot.

Use The Provisional Strategically

If you suspect that your ball has gone out of bounds, or may be lost, the proper thing to do is play a provisional. The provisional can be played until it comes to rest at a point that is closer to the hole than the point where the original ball was lost. At that point, you need to either find and play the original or play the provisional as under the stroke-and-distance rule.

Take advantage of this rule for the options it offers. Suppose that your first tee shot is a massive drive that appears to slice out of bounds. The provisional is much straighter, but noticeably shorter. You then can hit the provisional again before searching for the original. If that provisional goes in the hole for an eagle, or is even in a reasonable spot on the green, there's probably no need to look for the original. Take the one shot penalty and move on.

A side benefit of the provisional is that you get more practice shots. If you have a wild tee shot, the provisional offers an opportunity to rethink your swing before the next box.

Finally, on today's crowded courses, playing a provisional is the polite thing to do. No one wants to wait for ten minutes while you scour the ground for a ball, then (assuming you're playing by the rules) for you to return to the previous spot and play again.

Get Relief From Plugged Shots

A ball that's plugged in its own pitch mark in an area cut to fairway height can be removed, cleaned and dropped without penalty. When dropped, a ball must first strike a "part of the course through the green."

This rule is especially useful after a rain, when the fairways are soft. Note that this does not apply to balls that roll into another players' divot. That's just another "rub of the green." It also doesn't play to hazards.

Remove Loose Impediments

Sticks, pebbles and the like are loose impediments and may be removed any place on the course except in a hazard. If it can be moved, you can move it.

At the 1999 Phoenix Open, fans of Tiger Woods removed a half ton boulder that was blocking his shot to the green. That was permissible under the rules because it was not "solidly embedded."

Take care when moving objects: if you move the ball it counts as a stroke. Also, dirt doesn't count as a loose impediment.

Clean Up Your Path On The Green

The Rules of Golf permit a player to brush away (using his hand or a club) sand, dirt and loose impediments on the green, provided nothing is pressed down. A player also is permitted to repair ball marks on the line of the putt.

Make a habit of cleaning up your putting line. Putting is hard enough without having to worry about hitting a stick, leaf or ball mark.

Clean Your Ball

Any time you may legally lift your ball (for example, to get relief from an immovable obstruction or casual water), you may clean it.

It probably goes without saying that a clean ball performs better than one with clumps of dirt sticking to it.

Get Relief From Obstructions

In golf parlance, obstructions are artificial, or manmade objects. A movable obstruction would be a rake or a cart. Examples of an immovable obstruction are sprinkler heads, cart paths and out buildings.

If the ball comes to rest on an immovable obstruction or, if while taking your stance, any part of your body comes into contact with such, you are entitled to complete relief. Drop the ball one club length from the nearest spot that offers complete relief, as long as it's no closer to the hole.

Take advantage of this rule. If the ball lands on a cart path, the target spot is the closest one in which both the ball and your feet are off the cart path. And then you get a club length from there (no closer to the hole).

At the 2011 U.S. Senior Open, I saw a player take full advantage of this rule. His ball had come to rest on a sprinkler head just off the green, entitling him to complete relief. The nearest spot obviously was adjacent, but taking the belly putter, he located a drop spot that, when the ball was dropped, ended up on the green. He putted for a birdie.

For movable obstructions, the solution is simple: move them. If the ball moves when doing so, there's no penalty. It's just replaced.

If the ball comes to rest on top of a movable obstruction, the obstruction is removed and the ball dropped.

Get Relief From Casual Water

You'll often find casual water on a course after a rain. An area is considered casual water if the water is visible above the ground. Soggy or dew-covered ground doesn't count.

When your ball comes to rest in casual water, you are entitled to free relief. Find the closest dry spot and drop within a club length. The point of relief, however, can't be in a hazard or on the green. Otherwise, be sure to maximize your advantage here.

Get Relief From Abnormal Ground Conditions

Nature is messy. Golf courses are not perfect. Thus, when a player's ball comes into contact with "abnormal ground conditions," he is entitled to free relief.

Abnormal ground conditions include "ground under repair" and holes made by burrowing animals. Unfortunately, "ground under repair" doesn't include just any old area of poorly kept golf course. It has to be designated as such. There are a couple of exceptions: debris left by the greenskeepers which clearly intend to be hauled away counts as ground under repair, as does a hole caused by the greenskeeper -- even if not marked (tire ruts in the fairway?).

If you encounter any of those, you a free drop within a club length of the spot that offers relief.

After The Round

There's still some work to do after the last putt falls.

Debrief

When the round is over, take some time to review the good and the bad. Note the kinds of shots that didn't work for you. That'll be a starting point for your next practice session. As a positive reinforcement, congratulate yourself on specific shots that you played well.

Analyze your course strategy after a round. Imagine ways you could have saved strokes by making different choices. Identify trouble spots and think about ways to play those holes differently.

It's been said that the definition of insanity is doing the same thing over and again while expecting different results. A frequent playing partner has that particular affliction. Ignoring the wisdom of experience, he never varies his strategy on our local track. He's so consistent that he can accurately predict what will happen: "I always end up in that bunker over there," he'll say, right before driving into the heart of the sand.

I don't give advice -- that would be against the rules, and I might want the advantage in a future money game -- but if my friend engaged in some cold analysis, he could make some positive changes. On the hole in question, a fairway wood off the tee falls short of the bunker every time. That leaves a slightly longer shot to the green, but avoids the two strokes he typically employs to extricate himself from the sand.

A small change in course strategy can make a world of difference -- but only if recognize the need for change.

Go To The Range After A Round

Many of the top professionals make a point of heading to the driving range after a round to work out issues that they noticed. If you're in the habit of doing a post-round analysis, you'll surely find several things to work on immediately after the round.

Relax and Have Fun

Most of all, relax and have fun. You're not a Tour professional, and your mortgage likely doesn't rest on your ability to play.

You'll always play better when you're having fun.

finis

Thank you for purchasing and taking the time to read this book.

Acknowledgements

Special thanks to:

My family and friends for putting up with my addiction.

David F. Cline and Martin Lyle for their editing and advice.

Dennis Chall for introducing me to the game.

All the wonderful people I've met and played with on the course.

My many thousands of readers at GolfBlogger.Com

About The Author

John Retzer is the editor, writer and janitor of GolfBlogger.Com, the net's oldest continuously published independent golf blog.

###

CPSIA information can be obtained at www.ICGtesting.com
Printed in the USA
LVOW101650010712

288408LV00019B/85/P